This workbook

BELONGS TO

_____

OVERCOMING
A WORKBOOK

MICHELLE OBAMA

CLARKSON POTTER/PUBLISHERS
New York

Small
POWER

IF YOU'RE HOLDING this workbook, I suspect we are similar—like me, you are ambitious and striving to do better, be better, every day. Maybe you see every problem as urgent. Maybe you want to do big things with your life, to drive yourself forward with a bold agenda, not wasting a single second of time. But maybe, like me, you are also hard on yourself. Maybe you've found yourself worn down or overwhelmed or straight-up exhausted by this constant work. And I see you.

When you want to make a difference, when you want to change the world, your mental health will sometimes get in the way. And that's because it's *supposed* to. Health is built on balance. Balance is built on health. We need to tend carefully and sometimes vigilantly to our mental health. Your mind is constantly and imperfectly working the levers, trying to keep you steady as you figure out what to do with your passion, ambition, and big dreams, as well as your hurts, limitations, and fears. It may tap the brakes and try to slow you down a little sometimes. It may throw up distress signals when it senses a problem—if you're trying to move too fast or working in a way that's unsustainable, or if you're getting caught up in disordered thinking or harmful patterns of behavior. Pay attention to how you're feeling. Notice what's being signaled by both your body and your mind. And don't be afraid to reach out for help if you or someone you know is struggling. Many of us seek out professional support to maintain our mental health, talking to therapists or school counselors, accessing helplines, or consulting our healthcare providers. Please know that you are never alone. It's okay to pace yourself, get a little rest, and speak of your struggles out loud. It's okay to prioritize your wellness, to make a habit of rest and repair.

When it comes to wanting to make a difference in the world, I find that it can also be useful to break down those gigantic, all-or-nothing goals into their component parts. This way, you are less likely to get overwhelmed or exhausted, or crash into feelings of futility. None of this is defeat. What becomes defeating is when great becomes the enemy of good—when we get so caught up in the hugeness of everything that we stall out before we've even started, when the problems appear so big that we give up on taking the smaller steps, managing what is actually in our control. Don't forget to prioritize the things you can do, even just to sustain your energy and broaden your possibilities.

When you focus on the things you can control—often seemingly insignificant daily practices and activities, or your private thoughts—you regain what I like to call "small power." For me, the clearest form of small power I have is knitting. On days when my brain apprehends nothing but monolithic catastrophe and doom, when I feel paralyzed by *not-enoughness* and my agitation begins to stir, I pick up the knitting needles and give my hands a chance to take over, to quietly click us out of that hard place.

In knitting, when you create the first stitch of a new project, you *cast on*. When an item is finished, you *bind off*. Both of these actions, I've found, are incredibly satisfying—the bookends of something manageable and finite. They give me a sense of completion in a world that will always and forever feel chaotic and incomplete. Any time your circumstances start to feel all-consuming, I suggest you try going in the other direction—toward the small. Look for something that'll help rearrange your thoughts, a pocket of contentedness where you can live for a while. And it

> Any time your circumstances start to feel all-consuming, I suggest you try going in the other direction—toward the small. Look for something that'll help rearrange your thoughts, a pocket of contentedness where you can live for a while.

doesn't have to be knitting; almost any hobby or task or practice can be part of your toolbox for cultivating small power, so long as it works for you. Maybe for you it's playing tennis, or going for a walk, or building birdhouses, or saying a morning affirmation.

I'm not here to tell you that knitting (or any hobby) is a cure for anything. It won't end racism or demolish a virus or vanquish depression. It won't create a just world or slow climate change or heal anything big that's broken. It's too small for that. It's so small that it hardly seems to matter. And this is part of my point. I've come to understand that sometimes the big stuff becomes easier to handle when you deliberately put something small alongside it. When everything starts to feel big and therefore scary and insurmountable, when I hit a point of feeling or thinking or seeing too much, I've learned to make the choice to go toward the small.

The following section of this workbook is meant to help you find out what your small-power tools are, and to show that it's okay to be productive in a small way, to invest in endeavors that are adjacent to your big goals and larger dreams. And, in fact, it's more than okay—it's a critical tool for helping you overcome challenging times and remain more steady on your feet.

What have you faced recently that had you feeling anxious, or stressed, or lacking in confidence? Do you remember where you were, what you were doing, or who you were with?

_____

_____

_____

_____

_____

_____

_____

_____

_____

_____

_____

_____

_____

_____

_____

_____

_____

_____

_____

_____

_____

_____

_____

When have you noticed recently that you feel calm, grounded, or confident? What were you doing when you felt that way?

Moment 1

Moment 2

Moment 3

Moment 4

ONCE I'VE IDENTIFIED an imbalance in my life, something that's throwing me off, I first sort through my arsenal of fixes, trying different approaches to get myself back on track. A lot of them are small. Sometimes what I most need is just to take a walk outdoors, or to sweat my way through a workout, or to get a full night of sleep. Or to pull myself together and do something as simple as making my bed. Or literally just taking a shower and putting on some decent clothes. Other times, it's having a long talk with a friend, or it's spending time alone and writing down my thoughts. In some cases, I realize I just need to stop avoiding something—a project or a certain interaction— I've been putting off. Sometimes I find that I'm helped by helping—by doing even one small thing to make somebody else's day easier or brighter. Often, I just need to reset my mood with a good laugh.

It's these small rearrangements that help us untangle the bigger knots. It's the "just because" practices that nourish us. Small victories, I've found, can also accumulate. One little boost often begets another, one act of balance creates more. We can steer ourselves by degrees toward greater action and impact, sometimes just by trying one new thing, completing one seemingly insignificant task.

Go back and take another look at page 9. How many of the times you felt calm, or grounded, or confident were because you were exercising your small power? And were you doing it intentionally, or unintentionally? Reflect on whether you see that list differently by thinking of what you were doing at those times as tools, rather than incidentally nice moments.

_____

_____

_____

_____

_____

_____

_____

_____

How can you continue to exercise your small power in order to create more positive moments like these?

_____

_____

_____

_____

_____

_____

_____

_____

SOME "SMALL" ACTIVITIES *or projects can be immersive and calming, while others can be an additional source of stress or frustration, and the same activities can feel different for different people. I love knitting, but if I asked my husband to knit instead of reading a book or playing golf, he'd start to sweat.*

Fill in your "out of balance" states and your "small power" fixes—then match up which tools help you the most in each situation.

"OUT OF BALANCE" STATES

_____

_____

_____

_____

_____

_____

_____

_____

_____

_____

_____

_____

_____

_____

_____

_____

"SMALL POWER" FIXES

"It's okay to pace yourself, get a little rest, and speak of your struggles out loud.

It's okay to prioritize your wellness, to make a habit of rest and repair."

When you're feeling out of sorts—out of balance—how does that manifest in your life?

Think about the last time you completed a craft project or made something by hand. What did you create? Can you draw what you made here?

"In knitting, as with so much else in life, I've learned that the only way to get to your larger answer is by laying down one little stitch at a time. You stitch and stitch and stitch again, until you've finished a row. You stitch your second row above your first, and your third row above your second, and your fourth row above your third. And eventually, with effort and patience, you begin to glimpse the form itself.

You see some kind of answer—that thing you'd hoped for—a new arrangement taking shape in your hands."

Have you ever found that your mental health was negatively impacted while you were working toward a goal, even one you were passionate about achieving? Reflect on that experience.

Think back on some small things that changed how your day was going—whether for the positive or the negative—and list them here.

_____

_____

_____

_____

_____

_____

_____

_____

Are there any things you listed above that you could have been better prepared for, or responded to differently, if you had been in a more positive or calm mental state than you were at the time? If so, what would have been different?

_____

_____

_____

_____

_____

_____

_____

_____

_____

A DAY CAN feel hard and not-hard; a challenge can seem giant, and then maybe conquerable, and then two hours later, it's overwhelming all over again. It depends not just on your circumstances but also on your mood, your attitude, your stance—all of which can change in an instant. We get pumped up and knocked down by the smallest of factors—whether the sun is shining, how our hair looks, how we slept, how we ate or didn't eat, whether someone bothers to look kindly in our direction or not. We may or may not acknowledge out loud all the other forces that knock so many of us down, the social conditions shaped by generations of systemic oppression. But of course they are there.

> ... many things can happen beyond your morning to frustrate or overwhelm you or knock you off course, but when you buttress yourself against these forces from the beginning, you stand a greater chance of remaining resilient.

The start of our day is often when we can set ourselves up for how we confront these challenges; many things can happen beyond your morning to frustrate or overwhelm you or knock you off course, but when you buttress yourself against these forces from the beginning, you stand a greater chance of remaining resilient. However, it's easy to wake up and start the day with a critical thought. The mirror can be a scary place. Many of us find it tough to approach with any sort of ease, especially first thing in the morning. We can be reflexively harsh in our self-appraisal. We have often absorbed negative comments about our looks, messages that leave us feeling objectified, unworthy, or unseen.

Women are also consistently held to higher standards than men when it comes to grooming and style, requiring more elaborate, more expensive, and more time-consuming preparation before feeling comfortable heading to work or even just stepping out into a new day. I personally have plenty of mornings when I flip on the bathroom light, take one look, and desperately want to flip it off again. Face-to-face with myself, I'll impulsively start in on cataloging my flaws, seeing only what's dry and puffy, recognizing only the parts of me that could and should be better. In assessing myself, I instantly alienate myself. I start my day divided—one part of me a critic, the other a clown. One of us bites; the other hurts. The feeling is decidedly bad. It's hard to shake off. And that's what I want to talk about here—the possibility of starting kind.

I learned this small-power tool from a dear friend of mine, Ron. Every morning, without fail, Ron gets out of bed and smiles at himself in the bathroom mirror, then greets himself with a warm: "Heeey, Buddy!" I would guess that like the rest of us, my pal Ron often shows up tired and puffy at the mirror. He, too, has plenty of flaws that surely beg to be inspected and scrutinized. But what he sees first, what he chooses to *recognize*, is a whole person, someone he's genuinely glad to see.

Unlike a lot of us, Ron has figured out that self-loathing is hardly a good starting block from which to launch a new day. If you think about it, his simple message of compassion and approval is exactly the sort of thing many of us rather desperately try to wring out of other people—parents, teachers, bosses, lovers, and so on— and then end up feeling crushed when we don't get it. For me, part of the beauty of "Heeey, Buddy!" is that it's not terribly ambitious. It doesn't really count as a pep talk. It requires no passion or eloquence, nor any sort of belief that the day ahead will be stellar, full of new opportunities and positive growth. It is merely a friendly hello—two words delivered in a warm tone. And for this reason, maybe it's something more of us could try to do.

MANY OF US FIND *it difficult to look at ourselves in the mirror with acceptance, especially first thing in the morning. We can feel pressure to meet high standards for grooming and style, which women, especially, are typically held to. I am no exception. I have been trying, though, to wake up in the morning and give myself some sort of deliberately kind start. I invite a second thought, a more tender one, something intentional; often, it's just a quiet but grateful acknowledgment that I have made it once again to the starting line of a new day.*

Draw what you see in the mirror in the morning—then write some affirmations and kind messages for yourself that will help you start your days on the right note.

"Many of us spend a lifetime registering the presence of critical faces around us, feeling bombarded by judgment, asking ourselves what we're getting wrong, and internalizing the answers in harmful ways that stay with us for life. All too often, we turn the critical gaze directly on ourselves. We punish ourselves with *what's wrong* before ever having the chance to even glimpse *what's right*."

Now that you've prepared some kind starts you can offer yourself in the morning, I challenge you to use one of your affirmations every morning for the next five days. Then come back here and reflect on the experience.

_____

_____

_____

_____

_____

_____

_____

_____

_____

_____

_____

_____

_____

_____

_____

_____

_____

_____

_____

_____

_____

_____

In the challenge activity, how did it feel to offer yourself kind words rather than critical ones first thing in the morning? How does it change your day when you begin it by greeting yourself with gladness?

_____

_____

_____

_____

_____

_____

_____

_____

_____

_____

_____

_____

_____

_____

_____

_____

_____

_____

_____

_____

_____

"For me, part of the beauty of 'Heeey, Buddy!' is that it's not terribly ambitious. It doesn't really count as a pep talk. It requires no passion or eloquence, nor any sort of belief that the day ahead will be stellar, full of new opportunities and positive growth. It is merely a friendly hello— two words delivered in a warm tone."

You've been practicing the small power of greeting yourself with gladness, so let's refocus the scope of that power outward—think of and list some of the people in your life who are always happy to see you or who bring moments of gladness to your days.

Who do you
demonstrate
gratitude and
gladness for,
and why?

I'M GRATEFUL FOR

BECAUSE

I'M GRATEFUL FOR

BECAUSE

I'M GRATEFUL FOR

BECAUSE

I'M GRATEFUL FOR

BECAUSE

"How many of us remember the face of that one teacher, parent, coach, or friend who met us with gladness ahead of all else? Research shows that when teachers take the time to welcome students individually at the door, the level of academic engagement in the classroom goes up by more than 20 percent, while disruptive behavior goes down."

Recall a specific instance where someone showed you gladness in a way that changed your outlook on the day or on your circumstances. Write a brief letter to that person about the impact they had on you.

HABIT TRACKER | Now I'm challenging you to practice using your small-power toolbox—over the next month, track how often you take the following restorative actions (and add a few of your own unique habits and tools you've identified as well):

1	Dedicated time to a project or craft separate from my work or studies:	○ ○ ○ ○ ○ ○ ○ ○ ○
2	Called a friend:	○ ○ ○ ○ ○ ○ ○ ○ ○
3	Enjoyed time away from screens and devices:	○ ○ ○ ○ ○ ○ ○ ○ ○
4	Greeted myself with kindness in the morning:	○ ○ ○ ○ ○ ○ ○ ○ ○
5		○ ○ ○ ○ ○ ○ ○ ○ ○
6		○ ○ ○ ○ ○ ○ ○ ○ ○
7		○ ○ ○ ○ ○ ○ ○ ○ ○
8		○ ○ ○ ○ ○ ○ ○ ○ ○
9		○ ○ ○ ○ ○ ○ ○ ○ ○
10		○ ○ ○ ○ ○ ○ ○ ○ ○
11		○ ○ ○ ○ ○ ○ ○ ○ ○
12		○ ○ ○ ○ ○ ○ ○ ○ ○

"It's the simplest concept in the world, really: Gladness is nourishing. It is a gift. When someone is happy to see us, we get a little steadier on our feet. We have an easier time locking into our poise. And we carry that feeling forward."

NOW THAT YOU'VE filled up your small-power toolbox, you're ready to meet and overcome the stresses and uncertainties that life will undoubtedly throw your way with a bit more poise, armed with the knowledge that plenty of satisfaction and peace can be found in small things well within your control.

Remember that the bar is pretty low. Starting kind does not necessarily mean starting grand. You don't need to make any declarations about what you're going to do in a day, discover some deep new well of confidence, or pretend that you're invincible. None of this has to be done out loud, and it definitely does not need to be done in front of the mirror. You're just trying, one way or another, to box out the inner critic and push your gladness up front, to meet your own gaze—even metaphorically—with some small speck of warmth, to utter some sort of friendly hello.

Likewise, remember that small habits are undertaken almost because of their insignificance to your larger goals. Once in a while, you'll want to allow yourself the pleasure of a small feat.

This is the power of small, where the intermediate steps matter, where it can be relieving to engage in what's immediately in front of you, and where a start can more readily lead to a finish. This is how we move from *It's all too much* back in the direction of *I've got this*. It's how we continue to grow.

Comfortably
AFRAID

I'M GOING TO need you to tap into the tools you've collected for grounding yourself within your own small power, because we're about to take on something a little bit harder—and that's fear. First, I want to get clear on what I mean by *fear*. Most of what I'm describing here is abstract fear—fear of embarrassment or fear of rejection, worries that things will go wrong or someone will get hurt. I was fortunate to grow up in a reasonably safe and stable environment, among people I could trust, and I'm aware that it's afforded me a certain baseline for understanding what safety and stability feel like—an advantage not everyone is so lucky to have. There's plenty I don't see and plenty I don't know about the experiences of others when it comes to being afraid. I've not had to survive abuse, for example. I have not known war up close. My physical safety has been threatened from time to time, but thankfully never compromised. And yet, I'm a Black person in America. I am a female person in a patriarchal world. And I'm a public figure, which has exposed me to the critique and judgment of others, in some instances making me a target for rage and hate. I wrestle sometimes with my nerves. I feel a sense of jeopardy that I wish wasn't there.

Consider that the *Oxford English Dictionary* defines *jeopardy* as "danger of loss, harm, or failure." Who among us isn't walking around fully attuned to those dangers? Who doesn't worry about loss, or harm, or failure? We are all constantly processing our fears, attempting to sort out actual emergencies from manufactured ones. For the most part, the tools I'm offering in this section are not for actual emergencies—they're for softer ones that, yes, are sometimes manufactured. But such softer fears can still feel just as urgent and problematic in our lives. (If you're facing an actual emergency, unfortunately, you cannot workbook your way out of that one, and I recommend you put down this book and call the authorities who *do* have the tools to help you.)

The choices we make when feeling afraid, I believe, often determine the larger outcomes in our lives. When fear becomes paralyzing, when it robs us of our hope or our personal agency, that's when we slide into true disaster. Which is why I think we need to pay careful attention to how we evaluate our worries and learn to process fear. The goal is not to shed fear altogether. I've met a lot of courageous people in my life, from everyday heroes to giants like Maya Angelou and Nelson Mandela—people who, from a distance, might appear impervious to fear. I've sat with (and also lived with) world leaders who regularly make high-pressure decisions that both imperil and save the lives of others. I know performers who are able to lay their souls bare before stadium-sized crowds, activists who've risked their freedom and safety to protect the rights of other people, and artists whose creativity is fueled by a profound boldness. Not a single one of them, I would say, would call themselves fearless.

Instead, what I think they share is an ability to coexist with jeopardy, to stay balanced and think clearly in its presence. They've learned how to be comfortably afraid. What does it mean to be comfortably afraid? For me, the idea is simple. It's about learning to deal wisely with fear, finding a way to let your nerves guide you rather than stop you. It's settling yourself in the presence of life's inevitable zombies and monsters so that you may contend with them more rationally, and trusting your own assessment of what's harmful and what's not. When you live this way, you are neither fully comfortable nor fully afraid. You accept that there's a middle zone and learn to operate inside of it, awake and aware, but not held back. And with the right tools, you can even thrive in this middle zone.

When was the last time you felt afraid? Describe the situation.

_____

_____

_____

_____

_____

_____

_____

_____

_____

_____

How successfully did you face that fearful moment you described? What actions did you take—or not take—as a result of your fear?

_____

_____

_____

_____

_____

_____

_____

_____

_____

_____

Circle the types of abstract fears you hold—and if you feel any of these frequently, circle them twice. (Don't worry if you have lots of circles! I would, too, as learning how to be comfortably afraid doesn't make the fears go away; it only makes them easier to overcome.)

I'm afraid of:

EMBARRASSMENT

ACCIDENTS

AGING

FAILURE

CRITICISM

CHANGE

DISAPPROVAL

UNCERTAINTY

EMOTIONAL HARM

HUMILIATION

LOSS

LONELINESS

JUDGMENT

REJECTION

"Fear often arises as an innate response to disorder and differentness, to the intrusion of something new or intimidating into our awareness. It can be fully rational in some instances and totally irrational in others. Which is why how we learn to filter it really does matter."

IT WAS DURING Barack's campaign for the presidency in 2007 that I became even more intimately acquainted with my fearful mind, that ruthless, naysaying part of me that was sure nothing ever would—or could—work out.

For me, this was a whole new level of uncertainty. I am, after all, not a leaper or a flier, but rather a deliberate, rung-by-rung ladder climber. Like any good Capricorn, I like to get my bearings before making my next move. Up there, however, in the stratosphere of a fast-moving presidential race, there were no easy bearings to be found. The pace was too quick, the heights too dizzying, the exposure too great.

Over and over and over again, I had to coach myself not to listen to my fearful mind, the part of myself that kept saying: *You can't control this ride, so maybe you should get off.* Because if I did, I knew precisely what would happen: My nerves would fail. My faith would leave.

I've come to believe that the only way to learn how to be comfortably afraid is by getting to know your fearful mind. Why? Well, for one thing, it's never going to leave you. You can't evict it. It's more or less hardwired into your psyche and will accompany you onto every stage you set foot on, into every job interview you go to and every new relationship you enter into. It's there, and it's not going to shut up. Your fearful mind is the same self-protecting impulse you knew as a child—the same set of instincts that drove you to cry during a thunderstorm or scream bloody murder when forced to sit on a mall Santa's lap—only now, just like you, it's become more grown-up and sophisticated. And given all the times you've forced it to march through uncomfortable situations in life, it's pretty pissed at you, too.

Your fearful mind is basically a life partner you didn't choose. And to be clear, it didn't choose you, either. Because you suck, you're a failure, you're not very smart, and you never get anything right. So, seriously, why would anyone choose you for anything?

Sound familiar? It does to me.

I've lived with my fearful mind for more than sixty years now. We don't get along. She makes me uneasy. She likes to see me weak. She keeps a giant overstuffed file folder containing every mistake and misstep I've ever made and is constantly scanning the universe for further evidence of my failings. She hates how I look, all the time and no matter what. She doesn't like the email I sent to a colleague. She doesn't like the comment I made at the dinner party last night, either. She can't believe I say such dumb things in general. Every day, she tries to tell me that I don't know what I'm doing. Every day, I try to talk back to her. Or to at least override her with more positive thoughts. But still, she won't go away.

She is every monster I've ever known. And she is also me.

Over time, though, I've become better about accepting her presence. I'm not happy about it, exactly, but I do acknowledge that she's got real estate in my head. In fact, I've granted her full citizenship, if only because this makes her easier to name and thus to decode. Rather than pretending she doesn't exist or constantly trying to defeat her, I've gotten to know my fearful mind as well as she knows me. And this alone has loosened her hold and lessened her stealth.

Any time I hear the patter of negativity and self-criticism starting to get loud in my brain, when my doubts begin to build, I try to pause for a moment and call it as I see it. I've been practicing stepping back and addressing my fear with familiarity, offering no more than a half-friendly shrug and a few easy words:

Oh, hello. It's you again.

Thanks for showing up. For making me so alert.

But I see you.

You're no monster to me.

What does your fearful mind often say to you? Label each comment as "rational" or "irrational." How often is your fearful mind trying to limit you by focusing your inner thoughts on doubts and fears rather than on any potential or opportunity that might be in front of you?

Comment 1

RATIONAL / IRRATIONAL

Comment 2

RATIONAL / IRRATIONAL

Comment 3

RATIONAL / IRRATIONAL

Comment 4

RATIONAL / IRRATIONAL

Come up with your own mantra to repeat back to your fearful mind—how might you respond when you recognize that a negative thought is your fearful mind speaking?

ONE OF THE MOST *effective ways I counteract doubts and self-criticism is by focusing on understanding the nuts and bolts of the thing that I am afraid of.*

When, as a girl, I used to get freaked out during the violent thunderstorms that rolled through Chicago on humid summer evenings, my father would wrap his arms around me and break down the mechanics of the weather around us. He'd explain that the booms were nothing but clashing pillars of harmless air and that there were ways to avoid getting struck by lightning, like staying clear of windows and water. He never told me to get over my fear, nor did he dismiss it as irrational or dumb. He just used solid information as a means of unbundling the threat and giving me tools to stay safe.

Identify something you're afraid of, and then do some research! Diagram, draw, or write out what you've learned about that thing or scenario here.

What I'm afraid of:

What I know now:

MY MOTHER TOOK *a different approach than my father to helping my older brother, Craig, and me become comfortably afraid—her method was competence, and she led by example. She would sweep nasty-looking spiders off our doorstep, calmly shoo away snarling neighborhood dogs, and pluck flaming Pop-Tarts from the toaster when Craig and I had breakfast mishaps. Even half asleep in her bathrobe, she was a goddess of competence. And competence, I've learned, is what sits on the flip side of fear.*

Name people in your life, or public figures you look up to, who inspire you with their competence, their boldness, or any other way they face their fears. Explain what they've shown you about how to be comfortably afraid:

INSPIRES ME

BECAUSE

INSPIRES ME

BECAUSE

INSPIRES ME

BECAUSE

INSPIRES ME

BECAUSE

AT TIMES IN my life, I have felt both a little bound and a little provoked by the legacy of my two grandfathers, proud Black men who worked hard and took good care of their families but whose lives were circumscribed by fear—often tangible and legitimate fear—and whose worlds were narrowed as a result. Southside, my mom's dad, had difficulty trusting anyone who wasn't family and found it nearly impossible to trust anyone who was white, which meant that he avoided a lot of people, including doctors and dentists, even as his early symptoms of lung cancer went unaddressed.

My other grandfather, Dandy, was born in the Jim Crow South, lost his father early, and later migrated to Chicago, hoping for a better life yet encountering not just the Great Depression but also the reality that the North was dominated by the same racial caste system that existed in the South. He'd dreamed of going to college, but instead worked mostly as a day laborer, washing dishes, working in a laundry, and lining up pins in a bowling alley. Fixing, mending, carrying.

While I grew up only partially aware of what racism had cost all four of my grandparents—the doors that had been closed on them, the humiliations they wouldn't speak of—I understood that they'd had little choice but to live inside the limits imposed on them. I also saw the impact of those limits, how grooved into my grandfathers' psyches they'd become.

For many of us, this can be a heavy inheritance, carried by generations. It's a lot to try to push back against, to try to unlearn.

"Our
hurts
become
our fears.
Our fears
become
our
limits."

AVOIDANCE IS THE *adult equivalent of a child's shriek. Maybe you don't put your name in for a promotion at work. You don't cross a room to introduce yourself to someone you admire. You don't sign up for a class that's going to challenge you or engage in a conversation with someone whose political or religious views you don't already know. In trying to spare yourself the worry and discomfort of taking a risk, you're potentially costing yourself an opportunity. In clinging only to what you know, you are making your world small. You are robbing yourself of chances to grow.*

Identify something you've avoided in your past—a hard conversation or an opportunity—and imagine what might have happened if you had faced it head-on.

Consider your own family history. Did your parents and grandparents face circumstances that gave them reason to be fearful and restrict their worlds? Did they overcome significant challenges, though they likely felt afraid at the time? Have their choices in these situations had an effect on your own life and decision-making?

_____

_____

_____

_____

_____

_____

_____

_____

_____

_____

_____

_____

_____

_____

_____

_____

_____

THERE'S NO GETTING around the fact that our nerves will ride shotgun with us pretty much any time we approach the unfamiliar, any time we move into a new frontier and feel the stakes get bumped up as a result. Think about it: Who is utterly comfortable on the first day of school? Who doesn't bring a spoonful of fear to the first day of a new job? Or along on a first date? Who doesn't feel a jolt when walking into a room full of strangers or taking a public stance on something important? These are moments of distinct discomfort, foisted upon us routinely by life. But they can be thrilling, too.

Why? Because we don't know what lies on the other side of that initial experience. And the journey to get there might just be transformative.

However, when you learn how to be comfortably afraid and find yourself on the other side of things and experiences you once feared, you may end up in unfamiliar territory. There may be people who don't look like you there—or nobody at all who looks like you—and you may not know the rules or customs. And facing the types of fears and challenges that can arise when you've achieved more than you or your family have ever known or dreamed of takes a different level of resilience and preparedness altogether.

From an early age, I liked the feeling of achievement, of powering through challenges and pep-talking myself through fear. I wanted to live a big life, even if I had no idea what a big life exactly was, or how a kid from the South Side of Chicago went about getting it. I just knew that I wanted to aim myself high. I wanted to be excellent. I wanted to be a boundary pusher and a margin mover, but I was also not naïve. I was aware of the counternarrative that existed for kids like me. Already, I could feel the press of low expectations, this pervading sense that as a Black girl from a working-class community, I wasn't expected to amount to much or go very far.

> I've had to learn to establish a boundary between other people's worries and my own. I have to trust my instincts, remember my own center, and avoid getting too rigid with self-consciousness, too armored-up by anxiety or defensiveness.

What I've learned is that you don't easily lose your sense of being an outsider, even when you make it inside. There's a tension that stays with you, clinging like a fog. You can't help but wonder sometimes: *When will this get less hard?*

The challenge in leading a big life becomes trying to find ways to protect your dreams and your drive, to remain tough without being overly guarded, to stay nimble and open to growth, allowing others to see you for who you are.

You'll be well-served to lean on multiple tools we've talked about, plus a few new ones you may practice later on, to make it through whole. If you want to break barriers and knock down walls, I've found, you'll need to find and protect your own boundaries, watching over your time, your energy, your health, and your spirit as you go. So continue to return to your sources of small power, to stay centered and replenished and aware of what's within your realm of control. Continue to challenge your fearful mind and get more comfortable acting while afraid.

You will need to armor up as well. For me, preparedness is part of the armor I wear. I plan, rehearse, and do my homework ahead of anything that feels even remotely like a test. This helps me to operate with more calm under stressful circumstances, knowing I will most often, regardless of what happens, find some pathway through. Being organized and prepared helps keep the floor feeling more solid beneath my feet.

And yet I know that if I worry too much about such things and put on too much armor, I'll never manage to be myself. I've had to learn to establish a boundary between other people's worries and my own. I have to trust my instincts, remember my own center, and avoid getting too rigid with self-consciousness, too armored-up by anxiety or defensiveness. What I try to do is to keep myself agile, tacking back and forth between the familiar shores of caution and boldness. I live by the code I learned growing up on Euclid Avenue, the one that always put preparedness and adaptability way ahead of fear.

Think of where you are in your life today. What have you had to overcome to get here? Did you expect to be where you are? Did anyone in your life expect you to be here?

Have there been any times along your journey that you have let a fear, whether your own or one that was inherited or placed upon you by others, stop you from pursuing a certain path? Why or why not?

MY ARMOR IS MADE UP *of preparedness, punctuality, and competence—but also code-switching, power dressing, and humor; the ways we protect and guard ourselves against the abstract fears that confront us each day are varied because the challenges are varied, too.*

What components make up your armor? Draw or write them here.

"It's easy to be critical of one's forebears for their fears and their choices, to judge them for their compromises or hold them responsible for changes they were unable to make. The amount of armor being worn by an older generation will often appear rigid and outmoded to younger people, but it's important to consider the context. The fact that more and more Black women these days feel free to bring their full aesthetic into their professional lives, to wear their hair braided or in dreads to work, or that young people can sport body modifications or dyed hair without feeling othered, or that women have protected breastfeeding spaces at work, has more than a little to do with the work put in by people like the female partners at my former law firm. They had to prove their way forward, so that the rest of us might eventually have to prove at least a little bit less."

Which forebears made your current lifestyle possible? Did anyone who came before you make difficult choices or compromises that have resulted in your life being one that's freer, one where you can be less restricted or afraid?

HABIT TRACKER | This time I'm asking you to practice being comfortably afraid. Over the next month, track how often you use the following tools to overcome fears and handle new, stressful, or challenging situations (and add your own unique habits and tools as well):

1	Assessed whether a fear was tangible or abstract:	○ ○ ○ ○ ○ ○ ○ ○
2	Recognized that a thought was coming from my fearful mind:	○ ○ ○ ○ ○ ○ ○ ○
3	Used a mantra to subdue fearful but irrational thoughts:	○ ○ ○ ○ ○ ○ ○ ○
4	Investigated something I feared to better understand it:	○ ○ ○ ○ ○ ○ ○ ○
5	Prepared in advance to lessen fear in a new situation:	○ ○ ○ ○ ○ ○ ○ ○
6		○ ○ ○ ○ ○ ○ ○ ○
7		○ ○ ○ ○ ○ ○ ○ ○
8		○ ○ ○ ○ ○ ○ ○ ○
9		○ ○ ○ ○ ○ ○ ○ ○
10		○ ○ ○ ○ ○ ○ ○ ○
11		○ ○ ○ ○ ○ ○ ○ ○
12		○ ○ ○ ○ ○ ○ ○ ○

I KNOW FROM experience that challenging our fearful minds can lead to greater opportunities, and that our armor can often serve us—some of it will always likely be necessary—but I also believe that in many instances, it can be exhausting to walk around wearing too much of it, being too defensive, too prepared for combat. When you're hiding behind a mask, it's possible to become alienated even from yourself. When you're trying to stay tough and invulnerable, you may miss out on building authentic professional relationships that will help you grow, advance, and use your full set of skills.

There are costs associated with each choice we make. The bottom line is that when we spend a lot of time worrying about how we fit and whether we belong—if we must continuously contort, adjust, hide, and guard ourselves—we risk losing opportunities to be seen as our best and truest selves, as expressive, fruitful, and full of ideas.

This is the challenge and the drain of feeling othered. Many of us are left spending precious time and energy pondering those boundaries, the hard-to-parse difference between reach and overreach. We are required to think hard about our resources and how we spend them. Am I safe to express my opinion in a meeting? Is it okay to present a point of view or possible solution to a problem that's informed by my differentness? Will my creativity be seen as insubordinate? Will my perspective be judged as disrespectful, an unwelcome challenge to the norms?

Before we address those questions, take a step back and look at how far you've come. Maybe you've already made it into the room nobody expected you to be in. Maybe you're a student and you're on your way there. Maybe you're still figuring it all out. But wherever you are, you've completed a lot of tough self-examination in order to develop the tools to be more comfortably afraid while you face these bigger challenges. Next we'll practice how and when to remove your armor.

Source
CODE

HAVE YOU EVER felt like you don't matter? That you exist in a world that doesn't see you? Or that you exist in a world that sees only one thing about you?

Nearly everyone on earth experiences this sort of feeling at some point—that prickling awareness that you're somehow not suited to your environment, that you're being viewed as a trespasser. But for those of us who are perceived as different—whether due to our race, ethnicity, body size, gender, queerness, disability, neurodivergence, or in any number of other ways, in any number of combinations— these feelings don't just come and go; they can be acute and unrelenting. Living with them takes a lot of work. Trying to understand what causes them and what to do about them can be daunting, to say the least.

> It matters when we feel safe enough to show ourselves without shame and find ways to speak openly of the experiences that made us into the people we are.

It can be easy to presume that your differentness is the most visible part of you, the thing people perceive first and remember longest. Sometimes this is absolutely true, and other times it's not. The difficult part is that you will rarely know. You have little choice except to keep going, regardless. But the problem is, once you allow the judgment of others inside, it gets distracting. This is a hallmark of self-consciousness, a shift from thinking about yourself to imagining how people are thinking about you. And it can also become a form of self-sabotage, because now suddenly, you, too, are perceiving your differentness first. Instead of focusing on trying to solve the math problem on the board, you're worrying about how you look. You raise your hand to ask a question at a lecture, but you're simultaneously wondering how your voice sounds in a room full of people who are not like you. You're headed into a meeting with your boss, but you're second-guessing the impression you'll make, fretting about the length of your skirt and whether you should have worn lipstick.

You start carrying the load of your label, whatever that label may be. Your differentness attaches to you like a flag.

All this creates an extra burden, extra distraction. It adds another layer of required thinking to situations that for some might be casual, but for you now take energy. It can feel almost as if the world has quietly divided into two right in front of your eyes: those who have to think more and those who can think less.

> Our differences are treasures and they're also tools. They are useful, valid, worthy, and important to share.

Less visible types of differentness can also create an equal or greater mental burden—maybe there's something about your experience, your lifestyle, or your personality that you feel compelled to hide, or at least refrain from adding to the pile-on of potential things that others use to form their opinions of you. But the work it sometimes takes to detour around it in conversation can condition you to feel guarded and cautious, as if you're wearing an extra layer of armor. Maybe you have a parent or family member who was or is incarcerated. Maybe you grew up with a learning disability or speech impediment that you've worked hard to overcome. Or maybe at home, and among your friends, and in your community, you simply don't talk the same way people in your workplace do.

Amid all that effort and all that precariousness, you could be forgiven for not wanting to risk more by sharing a lot of your personal story. You could be forgiven for your inwardness, your caution, your layers of armor. All you're trying to do, really, is to focus, hold your balance, and not fall.

The challenge is to shift our perspectives and celebrate the value of differentness in ourselves and in others, seeing it as reason to step forward rather than back, to stand up rather than sit down, to say more rather than less. The work is challenging. It often requires boldness. And there are never any guarantees on how it will be received. But every time someone pulls it off, every time another tightrope gets crossed, we see even more perspectives begin to shift. It matters when we feel safe enough to show ourselves without shame and find ways to speak openly of the experiences that made us into the people we are.

Our differences are treasures and they're also tools. They are useful, valid, worthy, and important to share. Recognizing this, not only in ourselves but in the people around us, we begin to rewrite more and more stories of not-mattering. We start to change the paradigms around who belongs, creating more space for more people. Step by step by step, we can lessen the loneliness of not-belonging.

In this section, I want to give you tools for taking what you may perceive as your differences, or your weaknesses, and transforming them into the source code for your strength.

All around me, I see smart and creative folks who are gradually working their way into greater power and visibility, in many instances having figured out how to harness rather than hide whatever sets them apart. When we do this, we start to acknowledge all the contradictions and influences that make us unique. We normalize differentness. We reveal more of the larger human mosaic. We help make everyone's story a little more okay. But all that starts with becoming okay with your own story within yourself first, so that you can stand in a place of confidence and stability—and from there share your light with others.

As a kid—and as an adult, sometimes, still— I stood out in rooms I walked into for being tall. Once I went to college and joined the professional world and then political life, I stood out in many places because I am a woman, and because I am Black, and often even more so because I am both of those things at the same time. In what ways do you feel you stand out, or are different from your peers, in the spaces and circles you inhabit?

I STAND OUT IN/AT

BECAUSE

I STAND OUT IN/AT

BECAUSE

I STAND OUT IN/AT

BECAUSE

I STAND OUT IN/AT

BECAUSE

Pick one of the differences you identified on the previous page and reflect on how it makes you feel. What goes through your mind when you enter scenarios that make you conscious of this difference? When did you first become aware of it?

"Self-consciousness can take away your footing and erase what you know to be true about yourself. It can leave you clumsy and unsure, disoriented about who and where you are. It's as if the world has held up a mirror at an unflattering angle, showing you your unrecognizability to others, all the ways in which you don't belong."

Are there any situations in which your differences might actually be assets—whether you have used them that way or not? For example, as a teenager, my height would have been an advantage on a basketball team, or for reaching things on high-up shelves for my shorter friends, or in an apple-picking contest. Go back to the list of differences from a few pages ago—are there ways you can think of to pitch your differences as positives to start practicing how to reframe these traits in a new light?

WHEN I WAS A CHILD, *something that made my differences feel particularly alienating was that I couldn't readily find a set of heroes to follow. I struggled to find outlets for my height and strength. I may have been able to find a basketball team to play on, but something in me instinctively rebelled against it. (There was a kernel of self-loathing in my resistance.) I didn't want to gravitate to the one sport that tall girls were basically expected to do. Somehow that felt like a concession.*

Keep in mind that this was a different time. It was long before Venus and Serena. There was no Maya Moore, no WNBA, no U.S. women's soccer or hockey. It wasn't just sports, either. I came across very few people who looked like me on TV, in movies, or in magazines or books. On television shows, strong women who had a point of view were generally used only for comic relief, as mouthy or shrewish foils to the men. Black people were often depicted as either criminals or maids; almost never did they show up as doctors, lawyers, artists, professors, or scientists.

As a kid, I was striving toward some sort of existence I couldn't quite see. In life, it's hard to dream about what's not visible. When you look around and can't find any version of yourself out there in the wider world, when you scan the horizon and see nobody like you, you start to feel a broader loneliness, a sense of being mismatched to your own hopes, your own plans, your own strengths. You begin to wonder where—and how—you will ever belong.

Think about a person you look up to who shares one or many of the traits that make you unique, and draw that person or a representation of what they've achieved in spite of or because of those differences.

If you have struggled to find heroes who look like you, as I did, draw what your ideal hero would look like (even if it's just the most successful possible version of yourself—it's okay to be your own hero).

MY FATHER, WHOSE shaky demeanor and foot-dragging limp brought on by multiple sclerosis sometimes caused people to stop and stare at him on the street, used to tell us, with a smile and a shrug, "No one can make you feel bad if you feel good about yourself."

It was a brilliantly simple maxim, and for him, it seemed to work. My dad could shrug off nearly anything. He was good with himself, clear about his own worth, centered despite being physically unbalanced. I don't know exactly how he got to this place or what sort of lessons he'd had to learn along the way, but he somehow had figured out how to live unburdened by the judgment of others. This quality in him was so vivid, I swear you could spot it from across a room. It drew people toward him. It surfaced as a kind of ease—and not the ease that comes from privilege or wealth, but from something different. It was ease despite struggle. Ease despite uncertainty. It was ease from within.

It made him noticeable, visible in all the right ways. This was the source code to his strength.

He made a point of not holding on to pain or embarrassment, knowing that it wasn't likely to serve him, recognizing that there was a certain power in being able to shake things off, in letting certain moments go. He understood the unfairness was there, but he refused to be brought down by it, accepting that much of it was not in his control.

Instead, he measured his value by who he was and what he had—love, community, food in the fridge, two tall and noisy kids, and friends knocking on his door. He saw these things as success and as reason to keep going. It was evidence he mattered.

How you view yourself becomes everything. It's your foundation, the starting point for changing the world around you. I learned that from him. My father's visibility helped me to find my own. Whatever the signals in spaces that weren't welcoming to me were—whether people saw me as different, or unentitled to be there, or problematic in some way, even if what I was sensing was unconscious or unintended—I didn't need to let those signals in. I had a choice about it. I could let my own life, my own actions, represent my truth. I could keep showing up and keep doing the work. That poison wasn't mine.

Take a moment to reflect on my father's example and write about the ways you can measure your own value by who you are and what you have. What are the things that make up your foundation?

_____

_____

_____

_____

_____

_____

_____

_____

_____

_____

_____

_____

_____

_____

_____

_____

_____

_____

_____

_____

_____

_____

_____

_____

_____

"For whatever effort you make and wherever you get yourself, there may be people who will accuse you of having taken shortcuts or of being unworthy. They'll have an arsenal of phrases—*affirmative action*, or *scholarship kid*, or *gender quota*, or *diversity hire*—and they'll use them as weapons of disdain. The message is deeply familiar: *I don't see you as being entitled to what you've got.* All I can say is don't listen. Don't let that poison inside."

MY OWN TEMPERAMENT is different from my father's. I can be less abiding. I'm not able to shrug off unfairness quite the way he did, nor do I necessarily consider that a goal for myself.

In my memoir, *Becoming*, I wrote about how casually my high school guidance counselor seemed to brush aside my aspirations within ten minutes of meeting me, suggesting that I shouldn't bother applying to Princeton, since, as she saw it, I was not "Princeton material."

I was hurt and angry, destroyed not just by her words but by the indifference and speed with which they were delivered. She'd looked at me, evaluated me, and seen none of my light. Or that's how it felt, anyway. My path from that moment on would be shaped, at least in part, by that one remark—a single off-the-cuff sentence, uttered by a virtual stranger.

How many of us remain in a one-way dialogue with someone who demeaned or diminished us even decades ago? How many of us are still silently talking back to that person who tried to erase us from a place we were trying to get to? We return again and again to those moments, telling and retelling the story to ourselves, working hard to reattach ourselves to our pride. Those who diminished us live quietly in the margins of our minds, along with all our other despites—shrunk down by our excellence, the answers we've provided. They will be remembered only for what they failed to accomplish. Only for what they gave us to step over. In a certain way, they become fuel for our light and part of our source code, but their only power, it turns out, is to remind us of why we persist.

You take what you have and you march it forward. You find your tools, adapt as needed, and carry on. You persevere, understanding that there are plenty of despites.

Write about a time someone didn't believe in you or tried to diminish you to fit an unfair expectation. How did you feel at the time? What did this contribute to the source code that drives you?

"I learned that I could attach better feelings to my differentness. It was helpful to do when entering a new space, a kind of psychological squaring of the shoulders. I could take a second to remind myself of what, inside the walls of my own home, inside the shelter of my friendships, I already knew to be true. My validation came from inside. And it helped to be able to carry that power into a new room. In my own head, in real time, and for my own benefit, I could rewrite the story of not-mattering:

I'm tall and that's
a good thing.

I'm a woman and
that's a good thing.

I'm Black and
that's a good thing.

*I am myself and that
is a very good thing.*

When you start to rewrite the
story of not-mattering, you start
to find a new center."

Start to rewrite your own story of not-mattering. What can you say to affirm your own value and find your center?

I'M

....

AND THAT'S A GOOD THING

I'M

....

AND THAT'S A GOOD THING

I'M

....

AND THAT'S A GOOD THING

I'M

....

AND THAT'S A GOOD THING

HOW DO YOU know when it's safe, or the right time, to open up about your differences and let the people around you in on your despites?

One of the most humbling periods of my life was the months after I published *Becoming*. I was amazed by the number of people who showed up at my events, eager to connect over what we had in common. They came with their stories. They showed their hearts. They knew what it was like to have a parent with MS. They'd suffered through miscarriages, lost friends to cancer. They knew what it was like to fall in love with someone who sends your life swerving in a wild new direction. In opening my vault and shining some light on the times when I'd felt most vulnerable or out of control, I ended up discovering more community than I'd ever known. But it's worth pointing out that I came into that period of my life from a position of strength and security. I had left the White House behind and no longer had to serve as a political representative of my husband's office or of my country. I had also settled into myself as I gained more life experience, and I was ready to share my journey and let people in on how I got to where I was.

On a very basic level, it can be relieving when you take a calculated risk and let something out of the vault, releasing yourself from the obligation to keep it hidden or from trying to compensate for whatever might make you different from your peers. Often, it means you are starting to integrate the left-out parts of yourself into your larger concept of self-worth. It's a means of better understanding your own source code, and then sometimes revealing it to others so they can better understand you, too.

For some, this can be a very private process, done with the help of a counselor, shared inside only the safest of relationships. Sometimes it takes years to arrive at the right moment and set of circumstances to open up. A lot of us wait too long to begin even trying to know or give voice to our own stories. What we choose to share, what we show of ourselves and when, is not only personal but also inherently complicated—an often-delicate matter of timing, circumstance, and careful judgment. We need always to be mindful of what's at stake and who is there to receive our truth. There's no single rule of thumb that will ever apply.

What matters most is that we find ways to examine what's there in the vault and to think about whether or not it's serving us to hold it inside.

Is there anything about yourself that you have refrained from sharing with others? Why is or was that the case? If you have since shared this with anyone in your life, why did you decide to do so and what were the results?

"When someone chooses to lift the curtain on a perceived imperfection in her story, on a circumstance or condition that traditionally might be considered to be a weakness, what she's often actually revealing is the source code for her steadiness and strength."

YEARS AFTER I left the White House, my longtime personal assistant Chynna, who had joined my East Wing staff in 2015, requested a one-on-one meeting. I was terrified, because I was convinced she was going to quit; Chynna was not only integral to my life but also dear to my heart. Her job meant we were together practically all the time. We rode in the car together. We sat together on the plane. In hotels, we stayed in adjoining rooms. The miles we traveled made us close.

When we met, I sat braced for the bad news, but Chynna told me something else—that her father had gone to prison. And not recently, but when she was a young girl, twenty-five years prior.

After listening, I told Chynna that I thought she'd wanted to have the meeting to resign.

"No, ma'am, not at all." Chynna said. "I just needed to share that one thing with you. It felt like it was time."

We sat and talked for a while after that, both of us recognizing how much "that one thing" actually mattered. She explained to me that her entire life, she'd been ashamed to tell people that her father was incarcerated. That day in my office, I couldn't possibly reassure Chynna enough that her story—her whole story—was completely okay with me. I was grateful to know it. If anything, it only deepened my respect for her and everything she had achieved. These days, Chynna describes that conversation between us as having helped to unlock something in her, allowing her to shed some of that fear and let go of the sense she was an impostor in her own professional life. Inside the safety of our close relationship, the trust we'd built over time, she chose to let a certain part of herself out of the vault and into the light, a portion of her history that had always made her feel vulnerable, a piece of her despite.

While Chynna was at least partially motivated to keep this part of her story to herself because she assumed she was an "only," government statistics show that more than five million children in the United States have had a parent in jail or prison at some point; she was probably less alone than she thought.

What this means, though, is that a lot of us are left to assume that we're an "only" when perhaps we are not. Our vaults can leave us lonely, isolated from others. In keeping our vulnerabilities private, we never get the chance to know who else is out there, who else might understand or even be helped by whatever it is we're holding back.

Are there any ways in which you feel like an "only"? Take a moment to research some statistics about how many people in the country or in the world might actually be affected by something similar.

What did you find? How widespread is what you're experiencing?

Do you feel less isolated or invisible knowing more about how many
people experience something similar? Why or why not?

"Our differences are treasures, and they're also tools. They are useful, valid, worthy, and important to share. Recognizing this, not only in ourselves but in the people around us, we begin to rewrite more and more stories of not-mattering. We start to change the paradigms around who belongs, creating more space for more people.

Step
by step
by step,
we can
lessen the
loneliness
of not-
belonging."

SHARE YOUR SOURCE CODE; *embrace your differences. They're worthy mantras, but I can't suggest you rely on them without also addressing the inequity buried inside those messages. The work of visibility is difficult, and it's distributed unevenly. There's nothing fair about it, in fact. I happen to be well-acquainted with the burdens of representation and the double standards for excellence that steepen the hills that so many of us are trying to climb. It remains a damning fact of life that we ask too much of those who are marginalized and too little of those who are not.*

So please keep this in mind as I tell you to see your obstacles as building blocks and your vulnerabilities as strengths. I say none of it casually. I see none of it as simple.

My own experience has shown me that the risks are real, and the work doesn't end. Not only that, but many of us are already in a place where we are justifiably tired, cautious, afraid, or sad. But that doesn't mean your work won't count. Or that your story shouldn't be told.

Are there any spaces in your life where you feel you are unequally carrying the burden of representation or excellence? How does that feel, and how do you take time to restore yourself? (Can you rely on your small-power practices here?)

"When you do the work, you own the skills. They can't be lost or taken away.

They are
yours
to keep
and use
forever."

HABIT TRACKER | I am not going to ask you to track any habits here—the tools and practices in this section are more challenging, more personal, and often take more time to make a substantive difference in your life. The process of understanding your source code, sharing your differences, and opening up wider paths of belonging for others is neither speedy nor to be taken lightly. It involves work and effort.

1		○ ○ ○ ○ ○ ○ ○ ○
2		○ ○ ○ ○ ○ ○ ○ ○
3		○ ○ ○ ○ ○ ○ ○ ○
4		○ ○ ○ ○ ○ ○ ○ ○
5		○ ○ ○ ○ ○ ○ ○ ○
6		○ ○ ○ ○ ○ ○ ○ ○
7		○ ○ ○ ○ ○ ○ ○ ○
8		○ ○ ○ ○ ○ ○ ○ ○
9		○ ○ ○ ○ ○ ○ ○ ○
10		○ ○ ○ ○ ○ ○ ○ ○

Instead, return to your lists of some of the things that make you unique or different and some of the things that might make you feel like an "only." Fill those in here, and return to these pages to fill in a bubble whenever you find that you share some of these traits or circumstances with someone else. Over time, I hope you'll see this space fill and visually represent the connective power of opening up your source code to others.

○ ○

○ ○

○ ○

○ ○

○ ○

○ ○

○ ○

○ ○

○ ○

○ ○

WHAT WE OWE one another is the chance to build whatever platforms we can between us, even if they're made of small, seemingly insignificant connections, like the only foods we'd eat as picky kids or what our relatives' quirks are, and they still only get us halfway. This section isn't an argument for brazenly spilling all your secrets. It doesn't mean you need to do something big and public like publish a book or go on a podcast, either. There's no requirement to disclose every piece of private anguish you carry or every opinion in your head. Maybe, for a while, you just listen. Maybe you become a safe vessel for the stories of others, practicing what it feels like to receive another person's truth with kindness, remembering to protect the dignity of those who are bold enough to share in an honest way. Be trustworthy and tender with your acquaintances and their stories. Keep confidences, resist gossip. Read books by people whose perspective is different from yours, listen to voices you haven't heard before, look for narratives that are new to you. In them and with them, you might end up finding more room for yourself.

There's no way to eliminate the ache of being human, but I do think we can diminish it. This starts when we challenge ourselves to become less afraid to share, more ready to listen—when the wholeness of your story adds to the wholeness of mine. I see a little of you. You see a little of me. We can't know all of each other's source code, but we're better off as familiars.

Showing
UP

HOW DO ANY of us turn into adults, with real grown-up lives and real grown-up relationships? Mostly through trial and error, it would seem. By just figuring it out. Many of us puzzle out our identities only over time, figuring out who we are and what we need in order to get by. We approximate our way into maturity, often following some loose idea of what we believe grown-up life is supposed to look like.

We practice and learn, learn and practice. We make mistakes and then start over again. For a long time, a lot feels experimental, unsettled. We try on different ways of being. We sample and discard different attitudes, approaches, influences, and tools for living until, piece by piece, we begin to better understand what suits us best, what helps us most.

Our friendships and relationships are bolsters against the unsteadiness that comes from this constant practicing, yet they also require their own practice and can bring their own unsteadiness. This section will provide you with the tools to help you ensure that the relationships in your life are the ones that serve you and that you are well equipped to keep feeding those relationships so they can nourish you in return.

I am not someone who takes friendship lightly. I can be serious about making friends and even more serious about keeping them. My friends sometimes joke that I can be a bit of a drillmaster, even, when it comes to maintaining our bonds. They offer this observation lovingly and with an occasional hint of fatigue. And I get it. I accept both their love and their fatigue. It's true that I can be intense about staying connected with those I care about. I am a dedicated planner of group outings, getaway weekends, tennis dates, and one-on-one walks. I love always having something to look forward to, someone dear I'm expecting to see. For me, friendships are both a commitment and a lifeline, and I hold on to them as such, tightly and deliberately. I guess you might say that vigor is one of my Love Languages.

When it comes to your romantic partnership or friendships, I am not here to tell you that everything will be easy and perfect, or to reveal the ten secrets to a lasting marriage. I've always tried to help people see past the glittery side of my life with Barack and get a better look at our realness. I've made a fairly deliberate effort to blow holes in the myth that my husband is a perfect man, or that ours is a perfect marriage, or that love, in general, is any sort of breezy endeavor. I've written about how Barack and I went to—and desperately needed—couples counseling as we began to get prickly and distant with each other when our kids were young and we were both feeling maxed out. I've joked about all the times I've been fed up enough with my husband that I felt like pushing him out a window, all the regular and petty resentments I am capable of nursing, even now, probably forever. True intimacy can be aggravating; maintaining it does require that you have some tolerance for vigor, even if it's not your Love Language. And yet we stay.

> With our friends, we are always looking for very simple reassurances that we matter, that our light is recognized and our voice is heard—and we owe our friends the same.

I talk to young people sometimes who have made an art of embracing the casual and playing it cool, avoiding the fact that being real and vulnerable is a pillar of true intimacy. They haven't grasped the idea that there's room for depth and realness in all types of relationships. They may spend their twenties hooking up or pursuing a simple good time with lots of casual friends but not practicing the basics of commitment and good communication, the notion that it's possible to share real feelings and real vulnerability. They eat a whole lot of candy but build no muscle. And then when it's time to get serious, when they are imagining a family life and a more settled existence, they are suddenly, often frantically, learning these skills for the first time, realizing that there is little that's casual or cool about a lasting commitment or even a deeper friendship.

While casual acquaintances and easy connections can be an important part of your social ecosystem, what matters most for improving your ability to overcome challenges of all kinds is the quality of your relationships. It's good to be discerning about who you trust, who you bring close. With new relationships, I find myself quietly assessing whether I feel safe and whether, in the context of a budding friendship, I feel seen and appreciated for who I am. With our friends, we are always looking for very simple reassurances that we matter, that our light is recognized and our voice is heard—and we owe our friends the same.

The people who show up for us are the ones who allow us to build and nourish our own small power, help us to understand and process the things we fear or struggle with, and give us a safe place to be ourselves. I try to provide these same things for my friends now: a sense of home, a sense of safety and belonging, a sympathetic ear. Because whether we're celebrating, or struggling, or simply going through the day-to-day motions of our lives alongside each other, what matters is that we just kept showing up, in closeness, in commitment, in compromise, and even in fatigue. For me, it's all about showing up.

Take stock of
the current
friendships and
relationships
that are most
dear to you.
Who are these
people, what
role do they
play in your life,
and how long
have you known
them?

....

IS MY

.... ,

AND WE MET

....

....

IS MY

.... ,

AND WE MET

....

....

IS MY

.... ,

AND WE MET

....

....

IS MY

.... ,

AND WE MET

....

_____ IS MY

_____ ,

AND WE MET

_____

_____ IS MY

_____ ,

AND WE MET

_____

_____ IS MY

_____ ,

AND WE MET

_____

_____ IS MY

_____ ,

AND WE MET

_____

I WANT TO take a moment to talk about loneliness. Americans consistently report that what is missing from their lives is a sense of belonging, a simple feeling of being "at home" with other people. So many of us are looking for a sense of home. I understand that finding it is not easy, and people tend to feel embarrassed and shameful about acknowledging their loneliness, especially in a culture where self-reliance is considered a national virtue. We don't want to appear needy or inadequate, or to admit to feeling like we're on the outside of things.

According to a 2021 survey, one-third of American adults reported that they have fewer than three close friends. Twelve percent said they have none at all. So if the activity on the previous pages doesn't reflect a social life you're satisfied with, I hope you'll see that you're not alone in that. Take a breath, let it be what it is, and come with me through the rest of this section. I'm a firm believer that you can only start from where you are. Let's work together on some tools and practices that might help.

Loneliness comes into all of our lives at some point or another. When you are feeling lonely, what is the ideal, less-lonely vision of the future that you imagine for yourself? What type of relationships do you have around you?

What are some adjectives that describe the type of person you would want as a friend? Circle all that apply.

FUNNY   PUNCTUAL   ACTIVE

HONEST   BRAVE   COMFORTING   FUN

ADVENTUROUS   SERIOUS   INTROVERTED

SILLY   SPONTANEOUS   CARING   CALM

OUTGOING   DEPENDABLE   ORGANIZED

"One dip into Instagram will tell you that everyone's figured out how to be happy, loved, and successful—except you. Making a genuine, IRL, one-on-one connection with another person does help to counteract this. These connections are what open us to the actual lives of others, not just the filtered and curated existences we're likely to encounter online."

BEFORE I LIVED in the relatively confined world of the White House, new friends tended to pop up like daisies in my life, and I made the effort to cultivate them. If I encountered someone who seemed interesting, whether at work, or a holiday party, or a hair salon, I usually made a point of following up, getting that person's phone number or email address, proposing that we grab lunch sometime or meet up at a playground with our kids.

Nowadays when I'm talking to young people, I'll often hear them express fear or hesitation about exactly this moment in a new friendship—that hinge point when you make the move from *Nice to meet you* to *Hey, let's hang out*. They'll say it feels weird and awkward to pursue a potential friend. They worry about appearing too eager, thinking it makes them seem desperate or uncool. They are afraid to take that risk, worried about rejection. Their fears— no surprise—become their limits this way.

Every friendship has an ignition point. By necessity, it involves a deliberate extension of curiosity from one person to another, and I believe this is an offer you should never be ashamed to make. To say I am curious about you is a form of gladness, and gladness is nourishing. Yes, it can be awkward to express for the very first time that you might actually be glad to see someone if they were to meet you for coffee or maybe show up at your birthday party, but when they do show up and you do feel glad, you both get the gift. You're finding the light in another person, creating something new together. You are building a sense of home.

Think about moments when you might be missing out on potential IRL connections in your daily life—do you listen to music or podcasts in the dog park or on walks? Scroll social media while you're at the dentist or the salon? Run out of gym classes to your next appointment without introducing yourself to anyone? Write down what you do now, and what you could do differently to show up in a way that would make you more open to potential new friendships:

Moment 1

Instead of:

I could show up by:

Moment 2

Instead of:

I could show up by:

Moment 3

Instead of:

I could show up by:

Moment 4

Instead of:

I could show up by:

MEETING UP WITH

a potential new friend and going on a first date are remarkably similar—you will likely feel nervous and at least a little vulnerable going into both. What sort of first-meetup plans can you make to help take away some of the stress? Are there activities you've been dying to try that will help add excitement alongside the jitters? Is there a comfortable restaurant or coffee shop where you could schedule the meetup?

Draw the ideal activity or setting that would make you feel like you can show up as your best self for a first meeting!

FOR ME, FRIENDSHIP tends to happen gradually. It's a little bit like sliding down your car window to talk to someone new. Maybe at first, you're conversing across an opening of just a few inches—a little cautiously, careful about how much you share. If you feel safe, if your new friend is hearing you, you might lower your window another inch or two and share more. And if that's good, you open it farther, until eventually the window is fully down and the door gets opened and suddenly there's nothing but fresh air between you.

The simple truth is that making a friend involves taking a risk, which of course means swallowing a little fear. Friendship can be, at least at first, an emotional gamble—much like dating. You need to show something of yourself in order for it to work. And in showing yourself, you open yourself to being judged or even rejected. You have to be willing to accept the possibility that maybe, for any number of good reasons, you won't end up friends with this person after all.

Especially during my time as First Lady, it wasn't exactly easy to lower my guard when anyone new came into my life. But I also understood what would happen if I didn't. I knew I'd end up feeling isolated, a little paranoid, and stuck in place with a limited view of the world outside my walls. If I didn't drop my fears and open myself to new friends and new people, it would impact my ability to engage in my children's lives in a normal way. I wouldn't feel at home at school functions and potluck dinners. People wouldn't feel at home with me. And if others didn't feel at home with me, how would I ever be an effective First Lady? Staying open to people felt to me like a vital part of this new job.

At the same time, I wasn't a particularly approachable friend, living in the White House. Years later, when we could laugh about it, a friend I made during that time told me that knowing she'd be driving the family car up the stately access road that rings the massive South Lawn of the White House to pick up her child from a playdate with my daughter, she had gone out and gotten it washed. She'd also gotten her hair done. And her nails. Never mind that the instructions had made clear she wouldn't be setting foot outside the car.

I don't know at what point my friend grew comfortable enough to quit getting her car washed and her hair done ahead of her visits with me. But it started to matter less what either of us looked like, what sort of impression was being made. Slowly, we shifted into realness, no longer viewing each other across a gulf of nerves or expectations, happy to sit on the couch with our shoes kicked off. Each time we got together, we dropped our guard a little bit more, laughed more easily, spoke more earnestly about our feelings. The risks diminished. I was safe with her, and she was safe with me. We were friends now, and would stay that way.

Is there anything you do around new friends, or people you're newly dating, that you give up once you get to know each other better and feel safer together? How do you feel when you're able to get to that stage of a relationship?

What have you noticed newish people in your life giving up once they felt they could show up authentically with you?

"My real friends know what I look like without makeup on, and in bad lighting and at unflattering angles. They've seen me messy. They probably even know what my feet smell like.

But more important, they know my truest feelings, my truest self, and I know theirs."

BEYOND THE ONE-ON-ONE relationships in my life, I like to
think of my constellation of friendships as my "Kitchen Table."
My Kitchen Table is made up of all the people I show up for and
all the people who show up for me. It is a safe haven, a place
to rest in the storm. It's where you can pause the endless and
exhausting pursuit of overcoming everyday challenges and safely
dissect the barrage of indignities that comes your way. It's where
you can scream, yell, cuss, and cry. It's a place to lick your wounds
and replenish your strength. Your Kitchen Table is where you go
for oxygen so that you can breathe again.

No one person, no one relationship, will fulfill your every need.
Not every friend can offer you safety or support on every day. Not
everyone can, or will, show up precisely when or how you need
them to. And this is why it's good to always continue making room
at your table, to keep yourself open to gathering more friends. You
will never not need them, and you will never stop learning from
them. I can promise you that.

The best way to be a friend to someone, as I see it, is to revel
in their uniqueness, to appreciate them for what they bring,
receiving them simply as themselves. This sometimes means
letting friends off the hook for what they can't or don't bring. I
have active friends who want to climb mountains and take trips,
and others who are happiest to laze on the couch with a cup of
tea. There are some I'd call in a crisis and some I would not. Some

friends give advice; others regale me with stories of their dating lives. A few love nothing more than a great late-night party; others go to bed religiously at 9 P.M. I have friends who are excellent about remembering birthdays and meaningful dates, and friends who are scattershot about keeping track of that stuff but who will give you the gift of their sincere and full attention when they're with you in a room. What matters is that I can see and appreciate them, and they can see and appreciate me. They may show up for different types of meals at different times, but they all have their own unique place setting at my Kitchen Table.

Over time, too, a number of friends from different parts of my life have come to be close with one another, in part due to my drillmaster tendencies, my insistence that we gather as a group whenever we can swing it. Together, we have formed what I think of as a circle of well-wishers, a group in which we each are always rooting for one another's success. We announce our victories and get feedback on our challenges. We push through the hard stuff and nudge one another in small ways, through encouragement, through thoughtful listening. With my friends, the conversation is never finished. We are all guests at one another's tables, sharing the privilege of intimacy and honesty.

Draw what each of the important relationships in your life brings to the (Kitchen) table! What do their place settings look like, what dish did they bring, how did everyone show up dressed? Capture the most authentic representation of your table:

"Life has shown me that strong friendships are most often the result of strong intentions. Your table needs to be deliberately built and deliberately tended to. Not only do you have to say *I am curious about you* to someone who might be a friend, but you should also invest in that curiosity—setting aside time and energy for your friendship to grow and deepen, privileging it ahead of the things that will pile up and demand your attention in ways that friendship seldom does.

It helps, I've found, to create rituals and routines around friendship— weekly coffees, monthly cocktails, annual gatherings."

What rituals can you create to help you and your friends consistently show up for each other? Do you have any already, and what do you gain from this practice?

A COUPLE OF years ago, *black-ish* actress Tracee Ellis Ross wrote a touching tribute to her friend, the fashion editor Samira Nasr, on Facebook. She described how the two of them had met and bonded while working together at a magazine. Tracee had caught sight of Samira across a room and thought, "She has similar hair . . . I bet we could be friends." And it turned out she was right. They've been besties for more than twenty-five years now. "I couldn't do this life thing without her," Tracee wrote in her post. "I am a barnacle on her life."

I thought this was beautifully put. I've come to appreciate my friends as brighteners to my every day—but this is another apt way to think about them. If you've ever spent time by the ocean and encountered these bump-sized, hard-shelled crustaceans melded to undersea rocks and the bottoms of boats, you'll know there's nothing more stubborn or solid than a barnacle. The same might be said of an exceptional friend. If you're lucky, you might end up with at least a few melded into your life, people who become stalwart and unshakable, the friends who accept you without judgment, show up for the hard stuff, and give you joy—not just for a semester, or for the two years you live in the same city, but over the course of many years. Barnacles are not showy, either, which I see as also true of the best friendships. They need no witnesses. They are not trying to accomplish something that can be measured or cashed in upon; the substance mostly happens behind the scenes.

Think about someone who is a barnacle on your life—reflect on how that relationship transformed from a new friendship to the sturdy, trusted relationship it is today. Can you bring any lessons from that relationship to help deepen newer ones?

What are the most meaningful ways a friend has showed up for you?

What are the most meaningful ways you have showed up for a friend?

IN ADDITION TO friendships, the other type of relationship that people choose to show up for in their lives is romantic relationships. And people often reach out to me seeking relationship advice. They ask: How am I supposed to know when I've found the right partner, the sort of person who is worth committing to? Am I wrong to sometimes dislike my partner? How do I do a good job loving someone when my own parents provided a not-so-great example? What happens when there's conflict, irritation, hardship, challenge?

They remark on photographs they've seen of me and Barack together—the two of us laughing, or sharing a look, appearing content to be side by side—deducing that we enjoy each other's company. They ask how we have managed to stay both married and unmiserable for thirty years now. I want to say, *Yes, truly, it's a surprise to us, too, sometimes!* And really, I'm not joking. We have our issues, of course, but I love the man, and he loves me, now, still, and seemingly forever.

The honest truth is, I don't have answers to these questions or prescriptions to offer for anyone's individual challenges. The only love story I know is the one I happen to live inside every day. Yours will look different from mine, just as your conception of home and who belongs there with you will always be unique to you.

Only slowly do most of us figure out what we need in intimate relationships and what we are able to give to them. We practice. We learn. We mess up. We sometimes acquire tools that don't actually serve us. Many of us make a few questionable investments early on. We obsess, overthink, and misplace our energy. Sometimes we follow bad advice or ignore good advice. We retreat when hurt. We armor up when scared. We might attack when provoked or yield when ashamed.

You may also decide, as many do, that you are perfectly happy and fulfilled when not paired up with anyone. And if this is the case, I hope you'll celebrate it for what it is—a completely valid and successful life choice.

A lot of us, too, will unconsciously mimic the relationships we were raised around—whatever version of home we knew as kids—and this, of course, can work out either beautifully, or horribly, or somewhere in the middle. Real and lasting love, I think, happens mostly in the realm of in-between. Together, you are answering the question: *Who are we and who do we want to be?*

One thing I can share from my own relationship is that, just as with your friendships, the most reliable mantra is: Show up. Show up with curiosity. Show up with intention. Show up in the ways you would want your partner to show up for you.

If you choose to try to make a life with another person, you will live by that choice. You'll find yourself having to choose again and again to remain rather than run. It's an insane and seemingly against-the-odds proposition, if you think about it. And it doesn't always work. (It shouldn't always work: If you are being harmed inside a relationship, it is time to remove yourself from it.) But when it does work, it can feel like an actual, honest-to-god miracle, which is what love is, after all. That's the whole point. Any long-term partnership, really, is an act of stubborn faith.

My love with Barack is not perfect, but it's real and we're committed to it. This is what I think people pick up on in those photos: that tiny triumph we get to feel, knowing that despite having spent half our lives together now, despite all the ways we aggravate each other and all the ways we are different, neither one of us has walked away. We're still here. *We remain.*

If you are partnered or interested in having a partner, what qualities do you think are the most important for that person to have? Would you use the same adjectives you used earlier to describe the type of person you look for in a friend?

IN MY MARRIAGE, *it took us some time and a lot of practice to figure out how to work through our disagreements. Barack, it turns out, is an on-the-spot fixer. He likes to jump right in and try to hash out a relationship problem immediately when it surfaces. I, on the other hand, run a lot hotter and slower than my husband does. I boil over with irritation and then have to work my way gradually back toward reason. My brain will sometimes implode at the outset of a conflict, and the last thing I want to do is engage in some instantly rational, bullet-pointed debate about who's right or what the solution is.*

We've had to practice responding to each other in ways that take into account both of our histories, our different needs and ways of being. Barack has figured out how to give me more space and time to cool off and process my emotions slowly, knowing that I was raised with that sort of space and time. I have likewise learned to become more efficient and less hurtful while doing that processing. And I try not to let a problem sit too long, knowing that he was raised not to let things fester.

What's your argument style? Do you need time to cool off and take things at a slower pace, or are you more eager to fix things immediately? Identify the argument stye of your partner, former partners, and friends and loved ones, too:

	SLOWER PACE, COOLING-OFF PERIOD	IMMEDIATE FIXER
1		
2		
3		
4		
5		
6		
7		

How can you work with the people in your life to have disagreements in ways that respect both styles of responding to conflict?

1	
2	
3	
4	
5	
6	
7	

Does anyone in your life have a relationship that you admire and that might be similar to what you would like to create for yourself? In what way do you admire the relationship, and what about it would you change? (Remember that this isn't about judgment, and of course you don't know everything about anyone else's private life, but having positive examples of the ways we can show up for each other is a great way to identify what values are important to you.)

Reflect on your current relationship, a past relationship, or a close relationship with a friend or family member. Have there been any times you did not show up for them as well as you could have? What would you do in that same situation now?

_____

_____

_____

_____

_____

_____

_____

_____

_____

_____

_____

_____

_____

_____

_____

_____

_____

_____

_____

HABIT TRACKER | Challenge yourself to show up for new and established friends, partners, or family members in the following ways— and add some of your own rituals and practices that help keep you close with the people in your life:

1	Started a conversation with a prospective new friend:	○ ○ ○ ○ ○ ○ ○ ○
2	Participated in a friendship ritual (weekly coffee, monthly dinner, etc.):	○ ○ ○ ○ ○ ○ ○ ○
3	Went out of my way to do something special for a friend or partner:	○ ○ ○ ○ ○ ○ ○ ○
4	Shared something vulnerable about myself:	○ ○ ○ ○ ○ ○ ○ ○
5	Worked to understand a friend or partner's perspective during a disagreement:	○ ○ ○ ○ ○ ○ ○ ○
6		○ ○ ○ ○ ○ ○ ○ ○
7		○ ○ ○ ○ ○ ○ ○ ○
8		○ ○ ○ ○ ○ ○ ○ ○
9		○ ○ ○ ○ ○ ○ ○ ○
10		○ ○ ○ ○ ○ ○ ○ ○
11		○ ○ ○ ○ ○ ○ ○ ○
12		○ ○ ○ ○ ○ ○ ○ ○

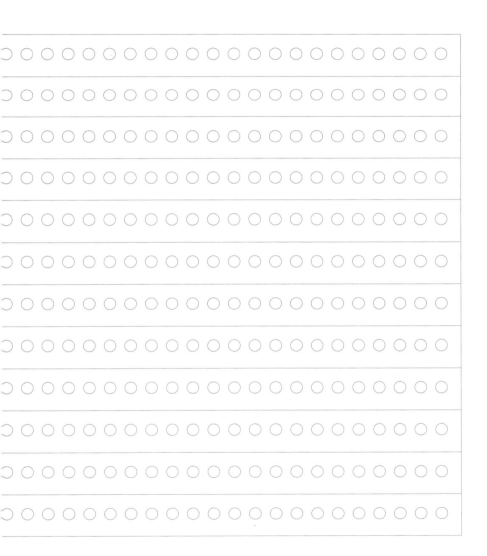

"DON'T DO LIFE alone," I often tell my daughters. Especially for those who live with differentness, it's important to create spaces where you feel safe and at home in order to survive. It's worth working to find people with whom you can remove your armor and shed your worries. With your closest friends, you can say all the things you've held back in other spaces. You can show your unbridled anger, your fear of injustices and slights. Because you can't hold it all in. You can't process the challenges of being different all on your own.

I am fully convinced that you will get further in life when you've got at least a couple of solid friends around you, when you're reliably and demonstratively invested in them, and they in you. And in any type of meaningful relationship, I have found that there is no right or wrong way to get through. There's no rigid set of partnership principles to live by, because the same thing won't work for everyone's life. There is only what we can work out between each other, day by day and year by year, through pushing and yielding, drawing from deep wells of patience as we try to understand each other a little more.

As long as you show up with intention and, yes, at least a little bit of vulnerability, there is both richness and safety to be found in other people if you're willing to extend your curiosity that way, if you can keep yourself open to it. Your friends and partners become your ecosystem—your Kitchen Table, the barnacles on your life—and by showing up for each other, we see each other through.

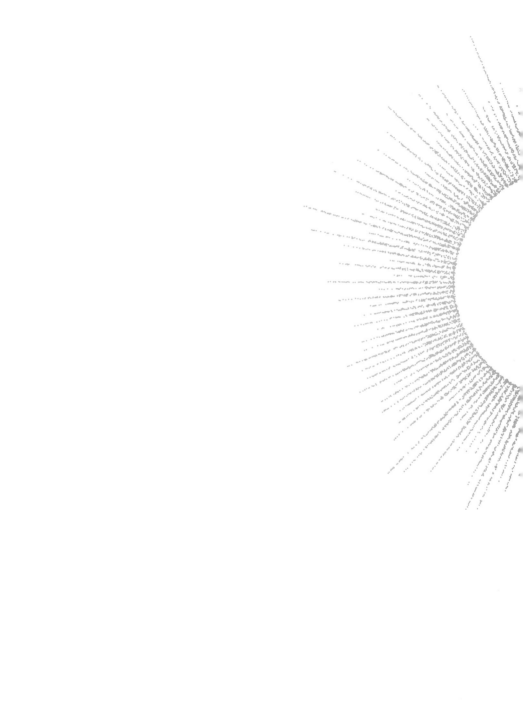

Those Kids
ARE ALL
RIGHT

CARING FOR YOUR kids and watching them grow is one of the most rewarding endeavors on earth, and at the same time it can drive you nuts. If you are in any way responsible for the life of a child, you are surely acquainted with this particular brand of fear and worry, the sleep-stealing torment of fretting about your kids—that haunting, lost-in-the-woods sense that you have somehow not done enough for them, or that you've done everything wrong, and they are now paying the price for your negligence or poor decision-making. It's something I believe many of us feel intensely and almost unremittingly, beginning with those very first moments when we take in the precious and innocent perfection of a little newborn face and think: *Please, oh please, don't let me screw you up.*

> Over the years, I've had one secret weapon to help overcome the tide of parental anxiety, though—and that's my own mother. She's been my backstop, my Buddha, a calm and nonjudgmental witness to my various shortcomings and, as such, a vital source of sanity.

My old friend, the fearful mind, would often rev right up with these parenting anxieties, triggering a cascade of doubt and guilt. (Have I mentioned that the fearful mind loves children? It knows all your soft spots and will go after them accordingly.)

Much as it is with marriage and partnership, the fantasy versions of being a parent sit at the forefront of our cultural imagination, whereas the reality is way, way, way less perfect. For mothers, the feelings of not-enoughness can be especially acute. The images of maternal perfection we encounter in advertisements and across social media are often no less confusing or fake than what we see on the enhanced and photoshopped female bodies—starved, carved, and injected with fillers—that are so often upheld as the societal gold standard for beauty. But still, we are conditioned to buy into it, questing after not just the perfect body but also perfect children, a perfect work-life balance, perfect family experiences, and perfect levels of patience and calm, despite the fact that none of us—again, truly none—will ever live up. The doubt generated by all this artifice can be potent and undermining. It's hard not to look around as a mother and think, *Is everyone doing this perfectly but me?*

Over the years, I had one secret weapon to help overcome the tide of parental anxiety, though—and that was my own mother. She was my backstop, my Buddha, a calm and nonjudgmental witness to my various shortcomings and, as such, a vital source of sanity. What she offered was perspective and presence. She was an engaged listener, someone who could quickly banish my fear to the back of the room or rein me in when I got a little "extra" with my fretting.

She told me that it's important to always presume the best about children—that it's preferable to let them live up to your expectations and high regard rather than ask them to live down to your doubts and worries. My mom said that you should grant kids your trust rather than make them earn it.

Her pep talks were brief and understated, in keeping with her character, but they were also reassuring. "Those girls are all right," my mom would say, with one of her shrugs. "They're just trying to learn life."

What she was telling me was that I, too, was all right, that I could calm down and trust my own judgment. This was always at the core of my mom's message. My mom gave me permission to share some of her tools with you in this section, but only if I attach the following disclaimer, which came direct from my mom herself: "Just make sure they know I'm not in the business of telling anybody how to live."

"In the end, the child you have will grow into the person they're meant to be. They will learn life their own way. You will control some but definitely not all of how it goes for them. You can't remove unhappiness from their lives. You won't remove struggle. What you can give your kids— what we can give all kids, really— is the opportunity to be heard and seen, the practice they need to make rational decisions based on meaningful values, and the consistency of your gladness that they are there."

What were the rules in your house growing up? How did you feel about them?

Do you have a different perspective on any of those rules now than you did as a child? In what ways might they have been put in place for you to learn from?

_____

_____

_____

_____

_____

_____

_____

_____

_____

_____

_____

_____

_____

_____

_____

_____

_____

_____

_____

_____

_____

Whether or not you're a parent, what are the basic rules you feel should be established for kids?

Rule 1

Rule 2

Rule 3

Rule 4

Rule 5

6

Choose four of the rules you listed on the previous pages—in each of the boxes, write how you would have felt about having that rule when you were a child. Would you have willingly followed it, or chafed against it?

For my rule #_____ ,

I would have:

For my rule #_____ ,

I would have:

For my rule #_____ ,

I would have:

For my rule #_____ ,

I would have:

MY MOTHER GREW up in a home that was orderly to a fault—my grandmother Rebecca took pride in her tidy house, her pristine glass coffee table, and her children who were seen rather than heard. But my mother always chafed against this restrained lifestyle, and in her own household, she took a very different approach. At home, Craig and I were permitted to be ourselves. Craig was a natural caretaker, and a bit of a worrier. I was feisty and independent. Our parents saw us each as different and treated us that way. They geared their parenting toward fostering our individual strengths, to drawing out what was best in us, rather than trying to fit us into any sort of preordained mold.

I tried to carry this same approach into my parenting of Sasha and Malia. I wanted them to feel both seen *and* heard—to always voice their thoughts, to explore in an unrestrained way, and to never feel like they had to tiptoe in their own home. Barack and I established basic rules and governing principles for our household: Like my mom, I had our kids making their beds as soon as they were old enough to sleep in beds. Like his mom, Barack was all about getting the girls interested early in the pleasure provided by books.

What we learned quickly, however, was that raising little kids followed the same basic trajectory we'd experienced with both pregnancy and childbirth: You can spend a lot of time dreaming, preparing, and planning for family life to go perfectly, but in the end, you're pretty much just left to deal with whatever happens. You can establish systems and routines, anoint your various sleep, feeding, and disciplinary gurus from the staggering variety that exist. But at some point, sooner rather than later, you will almost surely be brought to your knees, realizing that despite your best and most earnest efforts, you are only marginally—and sometimes *very* marginally—in control. You may have spent years captaining your own ocean liner with admirable command and antiseptic levels of cleanliness and order, but now you must face the fact that there are pint-sized hijackers on board, and, like it or not, they're going to tear the place up.

"As much as they love you, your children come with agendas of their own. They are individuals and will learn lessons their own way, regardless of how carefully you may have planned them. They will penetrate the bridge of your ship, put their hands all over every surface, and unwittingly break whatever is fragile, including your patience."

My girls revealed themselves to be very different children when they were young, and thus required different types of parenting—Malia was cautious, and often wanted our advice and input, while Sasha was feisty and wanted more independence from her parents. Compare and contrast your children's needs and personalities—or compare your own personality and needs as a child with those of one of your own children, one of your siblings, or any other child in your life you know well.

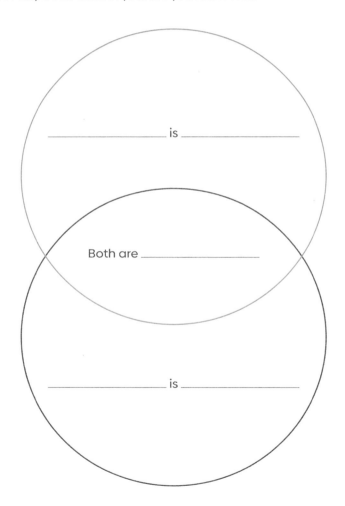

_____ is _____

Both are _____

_____ is _____

If you grew up with siblings, did your parents tailor their approach to your unique personalities and needs? Do you adapt your interactions with the children in your life to suit their individual temperaments?

BEYOND ALLOWING MY brother and me to be seen, and heard, and considered for our unique personalities, my mother also made sure that we were given some measure of agency early on.

When I was five years old and starting kindergarten, my parents gifted me with a small electric alarm clock. My mom showed me how to set my wake-up time and how to turn the alarm off when it buzzed. She then helped me work backward through all the things I'd need to do in the morning in order to calculate how many minutes it would take to get myself up and out the door to school. She was there to provide instruction, she'd furnished me with the tool, but the challenge of using it effectively became mine to figure out.

And I freaking loved that alarm clock.

I loved what it gave me—which was power over my own little life. If I ever did sleep through my alarm, or otherwise get lazy and drag my feet about going to school, my mother was not interested in doing any nagging or cajoling. She remained hands off, making clear that my life was largely my own. "Listen, I got my education," she'd say. "I've already been to school. This isn't about me."

I'm a firm believer that bestowing small and manageable responsibilities on children is a sign of trust, one that allows a child to either live up to your high expectations or else begin to learn about consequences in a safe and teachable setting.

What chores or responsibilities did you have as a child?

_____

_____

_____

_____

_____

_____

_____

_____

What chores or responsibilities do you assign to your own children? (If
they're little or if you don't have any, what might you start assigning kids
and at what age?)

_____

_____

_____

_____

_____

_____

_____

_____

Did you (or one of your own children) ever fail to live up to a responsibility or expectation that was assigned to you (or them)? What was the consequence, and what did you or your child learn as a result?

THE ALARM-CLOCK APPROACH was representative of an even more deliberate undertaking on my parents' part, and that was to help us kids learn to get on our feet and stay on our feet, not just physically but emotionally. From the day she birthed each of her children, my mother was striving toward a singular goal, and that was to render herself more or less obsolete in our lives.

Given how I've just finished describing how much I needed my mother's calming presence over the years, I suppose it's clear she did not fully get there. But it was not for lack of trying.

My mom made no bones about the fact that especially when it came to day-to-day practical tasks, her plan was to become as unnecessary in our lives as possible, as quickly as possible. The sooner that time arrived, the sooner she felt that Craig and I could handle our own business, the more successful she'd deem herself to be as a parent. "I'm not raising babies," she used to say. "I am raising adults."

It may sound scandalous to say, especially in an era when helicopter parenting has become de rigueur, but I'm pretty sure that most of my mom's decision-making was guided by one basic question: *What's the minimum I can do for them right now?*

This was not a cavalier or self-serving question, but rather a deeply thoughtful one. In our home, self-sufficiency mattered above all else. My parents understood that they were operating on a limited budget—of money, space, access to privilege, and, in the case of my dad's health, not just energy but time left on earth—which led them to be economical on all fronts.

My mom believed that her hands only got in the way of our hands. If there was something new we needed to learn, she'd show us a way to do it and then quickly step aside. We did a fair amount of this stuff imperfectly, but the point was we were doing it. Nobody was doing it for us. My mother wasn't stepping in. She didn't correct our errors or squelch our way of doing things, even if our way was slightly different from hers. This, I believe, was my first taste of power. I liked being trusted to get something done. "It's easier for kids to make mistakes when they're little," my mom told me when I asked her about this. "Let them make them. And then you can't make too big a deal out of it, either. Because if you do, they'll stop trying."

She sat by and allowed us to struggle and make mistakes—with our chores, our homework, and our relationships with various teachers, coaches, and friends. My mom remained quietly watchful over what was happening in our lives, but she did not immediately offer to fight our battles. A lot of what we were learning was social, developing skills to understand who we wanted to surround ourselves with, whose voices we allowed into our heads and why.

My mother helped me to learn how to puzzle out my own feelings and strategies for dealing with them, in large part by just giving them room and taking care not to smother them with her own feelings or opinions. Whenever I vented to her about a problem with a teacher, or a friend, my mom would listen and then she'd ask a simple question—one that was fully sincere and also, at the same time, just a tiny bit leading. "Do you need me to go in there for you?"

There were a couple of instances over the years when I did genuinely need my mom's help, and I got it. But 99 percent of the time, I did not need her to go in on my behalf. Just by asking that question, and by giving me a chance to respond, she was subtly pushing me to continue reasoning out the situation in my head. How bad was it actually? What were the solutions? What could I do?

This is how, in the end, I usually knew I could trust my own answer, which was "I think I can handle it."

How do you tend to support the children in your life in their problem-solving? Are you a patient listener and sounding board, or are you a solver? How do you decide which strategy is called for and when?

Reflect on the ways parental figures in your life did or did not give you the type of support you needed or wanted to solve problems. How has that influenced how you operate as an adult or as a parent yourself?

"Come home. We will always like you here."

"COME HOME. WE will always like you here." My mother said that to me and Craig not just once but often. It's the one message that stood out above all else. You came home to be liked. Home was where you would always find gladness.

I understand that I was lucky to know a good home early on. I got to bathe in gladness as a child, which gave me a distinct advantage as I grew and developed as a person. Knowing what gladness felt like, I was able to go out and look for more of it, to seek friends and relationships and ultimately a partner who helped bring even more gladness into my world—which I then tried to pour into the lives of my own children, hoping to give them that same lift.

I recognize that for many folks, "home" can be a more complicated, less comfortable idea. It may represent a place, or set of people, or type of emotional experience that you are rightfully trying to move past. Home could well be a painful spot to which you never want to return. And that is okay.

There's power in knowing where you don't want to go.

And then there's also power in discovering where you want to head next.

So the most important guiding question I will leave you with in this section is: How do we build places where gladness lives—for ourselves and for others, and most especially for children—and to which we will always want to return?

Rather than providing you with a habit tracker in this section and risk leaving you thinking only of the many chores and responsibilities that are disputed between parents and children, I'd like you to fill this open space with whatever the idea of a safe and loving home means to you—whether it's the one you had, the one you wanted, or the one you hope to build for your own children. Draw it, write about it—however you can best capture it, please do so here.

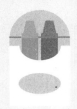

MY MOTHER OFFERED the best example I could have hoped for when it came to overcoming the biggest challenges of mothering and the inherent anxiety that incurs: She showed me that none of her parenting was tied to her own self-worth or ego, or done for bragging rights. It was not about her at all, she would say. She was busy trying to wash her hands of us, after all. This meant that her mood didn't rise or fall on our victories. Her happiness wasn't dictated by whether we came home with A's on our report cards, whether Craig scored a lot of points at his basketball game, or I got elected to student council. When good things happened, she was happy for us. When bad things happened, she'd help us process it before returning to her own chores and challenges. The important thing was that she loved us regardless of whether we succeeded or failed. She lit up with gladness any time we walked through the door.

My mother taught me that it was not about me. It was about my kids. And if I let them be the people they needed to be, and puzzle out their own lives with my loving support and structure and a loving home as the safe backdrop they could fall back against when they needed to, those kids were going to be all right.

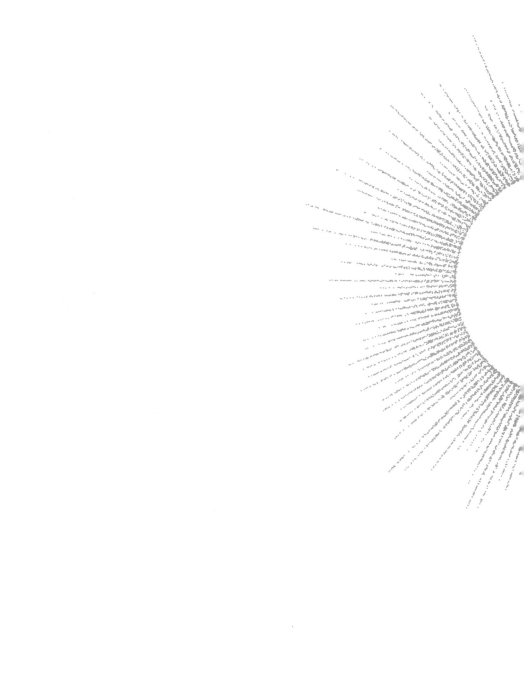

Going
HIGH

OF ALL THE questions I get asked, there's one that comes up more often than any other: What does it really mean to go *high*?

I first publicly uttered the words "When they go low, we go high" while speaking at the 2016 Democratic National Convention in Philadelphia. Truthfully, I had no idea that the phrase "we go high" would attach itself to me for years to come, becoming almost synonymous with my name.

All I was doing, really, was sharing a simple motto that my family tried to live by, a convenient bit of shorthand Barack and I used to remind ourselves to hang on to our integrity when we saw others losing theirs. "Going high" was a way to describe a choice we were trying to make to always try harder and think more. It was a simplification of our ideals, a soup pot full of ingredients, everything we'd gleaned from our upbringings that had been simmered into us over time: *Tell the truth, do your best by others, keep perspective, stay tough.* We invoke it any time we feel like we are being tested, as a reminder to steady ourselves when confronted by a moral challenge.

What do you do when others are at their worst? How does one respond when feeling attacked? Sometimes it's very easy to know, the answers feel entirely clear, and other times it can be more difficult, the circumstances more ambiguous, the right way through taking more thought.

I'm getting to "going high" last because you will need all the other tools we've worked on over the course of this journey to do this well. When you're encountering situations that require you to go high, it's going to be a lot easier when you have already centered yourself in your own small power, built up stable and supportive friendships and relationships around yourself, and learned how to confront fears as well as the full scope of your own personal story. Because make no mistake: Going high is work—often hard, often tedious, often inconvenient, and often bruising. You will need to disregard the haters and the doubters. You will need to build some walls between yourself and those who would prefer to see you fail. And you will need to keep working when others around you may have grown tired or cynical and given up.

How do we right ourselves inside a storm that shows no sign of abating? How do we find stability when the air around us remains unsettled and the ground seems to shift constantly beneath our feet?

I think it begins, in part, when we are able to find a sense of agency and purpose inside of ongoing flux, when we remember that small power can be meaningful power. Casting a vote matters. Helping a neighbor matters. Lending your time and energy to a cause you believe in matters. Speaking up when you see a person or group of people being denigrated or dehumanized matters. Showing your gladness for another soul, be it your child, or a coworker, or even someone you pass on the street, matters. Your small actions become an instrument for your own visibility, your own steadiness and sense of connection. They can help remind you that you, too, matter.

So when people ask me about going high, I explain that, for me, it's about doing what it takes to make your work count and your voice heard, despite the despites. And that becomes more possible, I've found, when you are ready and practiced with a full range of tools.

Going high is not just about what happens on a single day or month or inside one election cycle, either. It happens over the course of a lifetime, the course of a generation. Going high is demonstrative, a commitment to showing your children, your friends, your colleagues, and your community what it looks like to live with love and operate with decency. Because in the end, at least in my experience, what you put out for others—whether it's hope or hatred—will only create more of the same.

If you were familiar with my quote "When they go low, we go high" before, what did you think I meant? Has your understanding of "going high" changed in recent years, or after reading what I mean by it on the previous pages?

Think of a few instances in your own life when you had a strong emotional response to a situation and might have felt compelled to lash out and react right away with a "low" response. However you reacted, write a little bit about each situation and what the "low" and "high" possible responses could have been:

SITUATION		
"LOW" REACTION		
"HIGH" RESPONSE		

Reflect further on one of the situations you wrote about on pages 180 and 181—did you react and take the "low" way, or did you respond thoughtfully and "go high"? How might it have gone differently if you'd responded the other way?

FOR ME, GOING HIGH *usually involves taking a pause before I react. It is a form of self-control, a line drawn between our best and worst impulses. It's what happens when you take a reaction and mature it into a response. When you are confronted with a situation that elicits strong feelings, do you usually pause or react first?*

List some activities or practices you could use to help yourself pause before you react—what can you do instead of reacting right away?

"Going high is like drawing a line in the sand, a boundary we can make visible and then take a moment to consider. Which side of this do I want to be on? It's a reminder to pause and be thoughtful, a call to respond with both your heart and your head."

Draw some of your own lines in the sand—illustrate something that shows both the "low" side of an issue as well as the "high" one, the side you aspire to be on:

WHY, PEOPLE RIGHTLY wonder, *do we need to try to be so reasonable all the time?*

Any time there's another injustice, another round of brutality, another incident of failed leadership, corruption, or violation of rights, I get letters and emails that pose some form of this same question.

Are we still supposed to be going high?

Okay, what about now?

My answer is yes. Still yes. We need to keep trying to go high. We must commit and recommit ourselves to the idea. Operating with integrity matters. It will matter forever. It is a tool.

Going high is something you do rather than merely feel. It's not some call to be complacent and wait around for change, or to sit on the sidelines as others struggle. It is not about accepting the conditions of oppression or letting cruelty and power go unchallenged. The notion of going high shouldn't raise any questions about *whether* we are obligated to fight for more fairness, decency, and justice in this world; rather, it's about *how* we fight, *how* we go about trying to solve the problems we encounter, and *how* we sustain ourselves long enough to be effective rather than burn out. There are some who see this as an unfair and ineffective compromise, an extension of respectability politics, in which we conform to rather than challenge the rules in order to get by.

I can see how some think that reason leaves no room for rage. I understand the perception that going high means that you somehow remove yourself and remain unbothered by all that might otherwise gall and provoke you. But what I have learned throughout my life is that my actual power does not reside in my hurt and rage, at least as they existed in raw or unfiltered forms. My power lies in whatever I can manage to do with that hurt and rage, where I can take it, what sort of destination I choose for it. It hinges on whether or not I can elevate those rawer feelings into something that will become harder for others to write off, which is a clear message, a call to action, and a result I am willing to work for.

That's what going high is for me. It's about taking an abstract and usually upsetting feeling and working to convert it into some sort of actionable plan, to move through the raw stuff and in the direction of a larger solution.

I want to be clear that this is a process, and not always a quick one. It can take time and patience. It's okay to sit and stew for a while, to live inside the agitation caused by injustice or fear or grief, or to express your pain. It's okay to grant yourself the space you need to recover or heal. Because here's the thing: Emotions are not plans. They don't solve problems or right any wrongs. You can feel them—you *will* feel them, inevitably—but be careful about letting them guide you. Rage can be a dirty windshield. Hurt is like a broken steering wheel. Disappointment will only ride, sulking and unhelpful, in the back seat. If you don't do something constructive with them, they'll take you straight into a ditch.

My power has always hinged on my ability to keep myself out of the ditch.

As I I've said: Emotions are not plans. But your emotions, with reflection, can help illuminate what your plans should be. Think of situations where you've had a strong emotional response. What was the emotion, and what could it be telling you that you need to make a plan to address?

Emotion 1

I can make a plan to respond to this feeling by:

Emotion 2

I can make a plan to respond to this feeling by:

Emotion 3

I can make a plan to respond to this feeling by:

Emotion 4

I can make a plan to respond to this feeling by:

COMPLACENCY THESE DAYS often wears the mask of convenience: We might click on "like" or hit a repost button and then applaud ourselves for being active, or regard ourselves as an activist, after three seconds of effort. We've become adept at making noise and congratulating one another for it, but sometimes we forget to do the work. With a three-second investment, you may be creating an impression, but you are not creating change.

Are we reacting or are we responding? It's worth thinking about sometimes. It's a question I ask myself before I post anything on social media or make any sort of public comment. Am I being impulsive, just trying to make myself feel better? Have I tied my feelings to something concrete and actionable, or am I just being driven by them? Am I ready to put in the actual work involved in making change?

The problem with any simple motto, I suppose, is that it can be easier to remember and repeat (or to emblazon on a coffee mug or T-shirt, tote bag, baseball cap, set of No. 2 pencils, stainless-steel water bottle, pair of athleisure leggings, pendant necklace, or wall tapestry, all of which can be found for sale on the internet) than to put into active daily practice.

Don't sweat the small stuff? Keep calm and carry on?

Sure, yes, amen to all of it. But now tell me *how*.

Beyond the initial moment of inspiration or commitment, and beyond a period of feeling, reflection, or healing, it is often only with sustained action and intentional planning that we can truly make a difference.

Have you ever participated in some of the easier, lower-effort sort of "going high" that I described on the previous page—posting your view on social media without following it up with any action, for example? If so, take some time to write out here how you could move beyond that supportive stance and translate what you believe in into an actionable plan.

ONE OF THE things that always got my blood boiling was the hateful depiction of me in the media as no more than an "Angry Black Woman," which was especially vicious during Barack's first campaign for the presidency. If you were to believe some of the imagery and right-wing chatter, I was a full-on, fire-breathing monster. I walked around with a furrowed brow, perpetually seething with rage.

This unfortunately fit with a larger, more entrenched perception that researchers have documented in workplace studies: If a Black woman expresses anything resembling anger, people are more likely to view it as a general personality trait rather than as being connected to any type of inciting circumstance, which of course makes her easier to marginalize and easier to write off. Anything you do—any action you take—can be seen as stepping over a line. In fact, you can be dismissed as someone who simply lives on the wrong side of the line. All context gets erased when that label gets affixed: *Angry Black Woman! That's just who you are!*

When you're on the receiving end of labels like "Angry Black Woman" or any other hurtful stereotype, it can feel nearly impossible to want to go high when the very people coming after you have already shown just how low they can go. Such slights are a quick and efficient dismissal, a coded piece of bias that warns others to stay away, to retreat in fear and take their investments elsewhere. They overlook your riches, your vibrancy, your uniqueness and potential, and instead banish you to the fringes. And what happens if being stuck on those margins makes you angry? Well, then, your behavior now only confirms and compounds the stereotype, further boxing you in, further delegitimizing what you might have to say about any of it. You can find yourself voiceless and unheard, living out the failures someone else has prescribed for you.

It's a terrible feeling. And it's one I understand.

None of the negative headlines, of course, were true. Could I get pissed off about being seen as forever pissed off? I surely could, but who would that serve? How powerful would I ever become then?

Instead, I had to go high.

Think of the most hurtful stereotype or insult someone has ever thrown your way. Now conjure a better image instead—what positive thing do you wish for people to see you as or recognize you for? Draw or describe it here.

"Our rage is often warranted, along with our despair. But the question is: What are we doing with it?

Can we
yoke it to
discipline
in order
to make
something
more lasting
than noise?"

FOR ME, THE PROCESS OF WRITING *can be an incredibly helpful tool when it comes to going high. It's a means through which I am able to move through my emotions, filtering them into useful form.*

Writing things down or saying things out loud to a trusted listener has always pushed me to test my ideas in the bright light of day. It allows me to unpack my ire and my worries and to start seeking a broader reasoning. I'm able to sort out what's productive and what's not, landing upon a higher set of truths for myself. I've learned that my initial thoughts are rarely all that valuable; they're just the starting point from which I move forward. Seeing everything on the page, I then continue to refine, revise, and rethink, finding my way toward something with a real purpose. My writing process has become one of my life's most powerful tools.

Try it for yourself here—use the rest of this page and the next one to start writing about something you haven't quite figured out yet, whether a feeling, a plan, or anything that might benefit from more clarity.

I CAN'T PROMISE you that my tools will work for you, or that, even if they do, all of your worldly problems will disappear. But what I can guarantee is that uncertainty is a constant; we will continue to struggle, to contend with fear, to search for some sense of control. We won't ever necessarily have our bearings inside the historical moment we occupy, either. Are things trending toward the better or the worse? For whom? And how do we even measure? What might be a good day for you could be a terrible day for your neighbor. One nation might thrive while another suffers. Joy and pain often live in close proximity; they intermingle. Most of us exist in the in-between, following that most innate of human impulses, which is to hang on to hope. *Don't give up*, we tell one another. *Keep working.*

This matters, too.

Someday we will look back at this time we're now in. We will view it from a different historical perch, a set of future circumstances that we can hardly imagine now. I wonder what we will make of this time, what will feel recognizable and what will feel ancient. Which stories will get told? What changes will we have managed to make? What will we have forgotten and what will we have enshrined?

It can be difficult to talk about hopeful ideas—things like repair, restoration, and reinvention—in part because next to everything that has made us fearful and sad in recent years, all the tangible and concrete ways we have suffered, these can feel like comparatively abstract concepts. But progress requires creativity and imagination. It always has. Ingenuity is born of boldness. We have to be able to envision what's possible, summoning it from the unknown—whatever does not yet exist, the sort of world we hope to live in—in order to even begin to actualize a plan to get there.

We can't know for sure what the future holds, but I do think it's important to remember that we are also not helpless in the face of our worries. We are capable of creating change by design, change that's a response to flux rather than a reaction to it. We can operate from hope rather than fear, pairing reason with rage. But we'll need to renew our sense of possibility many times over.

When I was First Lady, any time I felt my stress level rising or my cynicism beginning to stir, I made a point of visiting a school or inviting a group of children to the White House, which immediately restored any lost perspective and helped clarify my purpose all over again. Kids, for me, are always a reminder that we are all born loving and open-minded, free of hate. They are the reason the rest of us maintain a thick skin and keep trying to clear the path. What practices, people, or experiences serve as your reminders of the good in the world when you start to feel low or dispirited?

As a Black First Lady, even though I was an "only," and I was having to help the world adapt and adjust to me at the same time I myself was adapting and adjusting to the role, my goal was always to do serious work in a joyful way, to show people what's possible if we keep choosing to go high. Where in your life could you do serious work in a joyful way? Are there ways you bring joy into your work already?

Going high is about learning to keep the poison out and the power in. It means being judicious with your energy and clear in your convictions when working with a limited but renewable set of resources. We fill and empty our pockets repeatedly throughout life. We earn, save, and spend.

Earn

What gives you energy?

Save

How do you preserve your energy and time?

Spend

What do you choose to direct your limited time and energy toward?

HABIT TRACKER | In many ways, the practice of going high is all about habits—or it's at least fueled by them. Repeated and sustained meaningful action over time is the surest way to work toward an important and noble goal, and making a habit of the steps you need to take will get

1	*Paused before responding, to go high instead of low:*	○ ○ ○ ○ ○ ○ ○ ○
2	*Identified an emotion rather than reacting to it:*	○ ○ ○ ○ ○ ○ ○ ○
3	*Used writing to clarify my thoughts and goals:*	○ ○ ○ ○ ○ ○ ○ ○
4	*Spent time doing something nourishing to restore my energy:*	○ ○ ○ ○ ○ ○ ○ ○
5		○ ○ ○ ○ ○ ○ ○ ○
6		○ ○ ○ ○ ○ ○ ○ ○
7		○ ○ ○ ○ ○ ○ ○ ○
8		○ ○ ○ ○ ○ ○ ○ ○
9		○ ○ ○ ○ ○ ○ ○ ○
10		○ ○ ○ ○ ○ ○ ○ ○
11		○ ○ ○ ○ ○ ○ ○ ○
12		○ ○ ○ ○ ○ ○ ○ ○

you quite far. Write in your own unique habits that'll get you well on your way to achieving your larger goals alongside the tools I've shared for helping to stabilize you on your journey there:

○ ○

○ ○

○ ○

○ ○

○ ○

○ ○

○ ○

○ ○

○ ○

○ ○

○ ○

○ ○

THERE'S A TYPE of question I get often from young people who are feeling both motivated and impatient, fed up with the way things are. It's a question that gets at the nature of activism, resistance, and change more generally: How much do we abide by and how much do we reject? Do we tear down our systems or try to stay patient and reform them from the inside? Are we more effective agitating for change at the margins or inside the mainstream? What does true boldness look like? When does civility become an excuse for inaction?

These are not new questions. It's not a new debate. Each generation rediscovers it on its own. And the answers aren't straightforward. Which is why the debate stays fresh, the questions remain open, and, if you're lucky, why your own kids and grandkids will come to you someday, burning with passion, frustrated and impatient and ready to challenge, pondering the very margins you tried to widen for them, asking these same questions all over again.

So what about going high? Can we still? *Should* we still? In the face of all that's grim and unrelenting and anguished and infuriating about the world we live in, does it even work? Where does integrity get us in hard times?

I hear all the raw feelings these questions come wrapped in—the anger and disappointment, the hurt and panic that so many of us understandably feel. But keep in mind how quickly they can take us into the ditch.

What I want to say, what I will always want to remind you of, is this: Going high is a commitment, and not a particularly glamorous one, to keep moving forward. It only works when we do the work.

A motto stays hollow if we only repeat it and put it on products we can sell on Etsy. We need to embody it, pour ourselves into it—pour our frustration and hurt into it, even. What I want to say, then, is stay vigorous and faithful, humble and empathetic. Tell the truth, do your best by others, keep perspective, understand history and context. Stay prudent, stay tough, and stay outraged.

But more than anything, don't forget to do the work.

I'll continue answering the question. And I'll stick with my same answer about whether going high matters.

It's yes, always yes.

NOTES

32   *when teachers take the time* Clayton R. Cook et al., "Positive Greetings at the Door: Evaluation of a Low-Cost, High-Yield Proactive Classroom Management Strategy," *Journal of Positive Behavior Interventions* 20, no. 3 (2018): 149-59, doi.org/10.1177/1098300717753831.

112   *a 2021 survey* Daniel A. Cox, "The State of American Friendship: Change, Challenges, and Loss," June 8, 2021, Survey Center on American Life, www.americansurveycenter.org/research/the-state-of-american-friendship-change-challenges-and-loss/.

191   *researchers have documented* Daphna Motro et al., "Race and Reactions to Women's Expressions of Anger at Work: Examining the Effects of the 'Angry Black Woman' Stereotype," *Journal of Applied Psychology* 107, no. 1 (2021): 142-52, doi.org/10.1037/apl0000884.

Published in the United States by Clarkson Potter/Publishers,
an imprint of the Crown Publishing Group, a division of
Penguin Random House LLC, New York.
ClarksonPotter.com

CLARKSON POTTER is a trademark and POTTER with colophon
is a registered trademark of Penguin Random House LLC.

Selected material originally appeared in *The Light We Carry*
by Michelle Obama, published by Crown, an imprint of Penguin
Random House LLC, New York, in 2022, copyright © 2022 by
Michelle Obama.

ISBN 978-0-593-23749-6

Printed in Malaysia

Illustrations by Danielle Deschenes
Shutterstock art assets © pages 4, 38, 66, 68, 104, 105–106, 120,
128–129, 133, 146, 147–148, 175–176, 186, 189, and 191

Editor: Madison Jacobs
Designer: Danielle Deschenes
Production editor: Abby Oladipo
Production manager: Luisa Francavilla
Copyeditor: Sibylle Kazeroid
Proofreaders: Diana Drew and Sarah Rutledge
Compositor: Zoe Tokushige
Publicist: Penny Simon
Marketer: Julie Cepler

10 9 8 7 6 5 4 3 2 1

First Edition